# *fresh* at home

RUTH TAL BROWN (LEFT) AND JENNIFER HOUSTON

## RUTH TAL BROWN
### FOUNDER AND CO-OWNER

After travelling the world for seven years, Ruth Tal Brown returned to Toronto to attend Ryerson Polytechnic and the University of Toronto. Her studies, however, were short-lived. Inspired by the radical improvement in her health after completing a series of intensive juice fasts and shifting to a vegan diet, Ruth quit school and set out to open a vegetarian food and juice bar that would be a haven for all those interested in a healthier diet.

Juice for Life began as a travelling juice bar, with booths at events such as the Lollapolooza Rock Festival, Caribana Caribbean Festival, Kumbaya Aids Benefit, various health lectures and the Toronto Vegetarian Food Fair. Ruth's first location, a seasonal juice bar, opened at the Bamboo Club in 1991. One year later, she moved to a permanent location in the newly renovated Queen Street Market, where she developed the signature juices and dishes that form the core of the Juice for Life concept. In 1995 Ruth opened the Bloor Street Juice for Life restaurant. In June 1998 she opened the Queen Street Café, a larger improved version of the Queen Street Market. Both locations have received numerous awards over the years for "Best Vegetarian Restaurant" from the local Toronto press. Juice for Life was also selected as "Best Juice Bar in North America" as featured on the Food Network and was named one of the top 20 most influential restaurants in Toronto by *Now* magazine.

Dubbed the "Queen of the Canadian Juice Bar Scene" by *The Globe and Mail*, Ruth became a national bestselling author with the release of her first cookbook, *Juice for Life: Modern Food and Luscious Juice*, in 2001. The following year, Ruth changed the restaurants' name to Fresh by Juice for Life and opened the third downtown Toronto location in the Queen West gallery district, which has won international, national and provincial architectural and design awards. In August 2003, Ruth taped 13 segments for *Flex*, a Raptors/NBA TV show featuring dishes and juices from the Fresh menus.

## JENNIFER HOUSTON
### HEAD CHEF AND CO-OWNER

After graduating from Queen's University in Kingston, Jennifer Houston worked in various jobs in the food and beverage industry for five years. During this time, Jennifer discovered her talent lay in the world of culinary arts and professional kitchens. She graduated, first in her class, from chef training at George Brown College. In 1997, Jennifer was introduced to professional vegetarian cooking while living in Scotland.

Upon returning to Canada, Jennifer was hired as a sous chef at the Bloor Street Juice for Life restaurant. Soon after, she was promoted to the position of head chef and chief purchasing officer for both locations.

In 2000, Jennifer became a partner in the business. In September 2002, she and her partners opened the third Fresh by Juice for Life location. Jennifer now oversees all three kitchens.

## Also by Ruth Tal Brown

**Juice for Life: Modern Food and Luscious Juice**

Ruth Tal Brown * Jennifer Houston

# *fresh* at home

## EVERYDAY VEGETARIAN COOKING

PENGUIN
CANADA

PENGUIN CANADA

Published by the Penguin Group

Penguin Group (Canada), 90 Eglinton Avenue East, Suite 700, Toronto, Ontario, Canada M4P 2Y3 (a division of Pearson Penguin Canada Inc.)

Penguin Group (USA) Inc., 375 Hudson Street, New York, New York 10014, U.S.A.
Penguin Books Ltd, 80 Strand, London WC2R 0RL, England
Penguin Ireland, 25 St Stephen's Green, Dublin 2, Ireland (a division of Penguin Books Ltd)
Penguin Group (Australia), 250 Camberwell Road, Camberwell, Victoria 3124, Australia (a division of Pearson Australia Group Pty Ltd)
Penguin Books India Pvt Ltd, 11 Community Centre, Panchsheel Park, New Delhi – 110 017, India
Penguin Group (NZ), cnr Airborne and Rosedale Roads, Albany, Auckland 1310, New Zealand (a division of Pearson New Zealand Ltd)
Penguin Books (South Africa) (Pty) Ltd, 24 Sturdee Avenue, Rosebank, Johannesburg 2196, South Africa

Penguin Books Ltd, Registered Offices: 80 Strand, London WC2R 0RL, England

First published 2004

(WEB)  10 9 8 7 6

Manufactured in Canada.

_____

NATIONAL LIBRARY OF CANADA CATALOGUING IN PUBLICATION

Brown, Ruth Tal
     Fresh at home : everyday vegetarian cooking / Ruth Tal Brown and Jennifer Houston

Includes bibliographical references and index.
ISBN 0-14-301598-2

     1. Vegetarian cookery. I. Houston, Jennifer, 1968– II. Title.

TX837.B838 2004    641.5'636    C2003-906799-8

_____

Visit the Penguin Group (Canada) website at **www.penguin.ca**

For my brother, Ronnie. Because every day you inspire me.
For your brave heart, integrity and adventurous spirit.

*RTB*


For my parents, Wayne and Barbara Houston, who have shown me
unwavering love and support for as long as I can remember. And for teaching me
that the harder you work, the luckier you get.

*JLH*

# contents

# foreword

In the history of eating, there has never been a better time to own this book. Before I explain my reasons, I'd like to write candidly about Ruth Tal Brown: the founder of Fresh by Juice for Life.

Getting to know Ruth wasn't easy. There was a time when I actually had to fold her laundry in an effort to get her to accept me as a pal.

I first saw Ruth when she was setting up her juice bar in Toronto's diminutive Queen Street West Market back in 1992. I distinctly remember saying to myself, "Wow! What a beautiful, vibrant woman!" I had no idea who she was or what she was doing, although there did seem to be a lot of grinding and mashing of fruits and vegetables going on. But what style of cuisine was it? And who were all those exotic devotees who hung around awaiting her concoctions? Was it a cult? Despite being a wee bit intimidated, I often detoured through the market on my way home, specifically hoping to catch a glimpse of the beautiful Ruth.

Not long after my first Ruth sighting, I was both shocked and thrilled to discover that the family living upstairs had moved out and Ruth and a roommate had moved in. Here was fate saying, "Carlo, I've done my bit . . ."

So, I set to work. Sensing a reticence on the part of my new neighbour, I opted for a slow, sensitive approach. I began with music, making sure that only sophisticated, soothing melodies wafted from my apartment. I purchased unstructured soft cotton trousers from Little India so as to appear more . . . er . . . Little Indian. My coup de grâce, however, occurred in our shared laundry space. Sometimes I would find things in the dryer and, in an inspired moment, the above-mentioned laundry folding took place (naturally, I was careful to avoid folding anything provocative or frilly). How could she resist?

Well, I am pleased to say that she did not. Ruth soon became an excellent friend and remains so. She has taught me a great deal about the incredible advantages of fresh juices and vegetarian cooking. I am proud to have seen her expand her business and get married.

And I'm particularly proud that she asked me to write this foreword.

Now, about this book. More and more people I speak to are looking for alternative diets—not fad diets or quick weight-loss diets, but diets meant to last a lifetime. Many I know have gleefully divulged that they are eating less meat, dairy products, processed flour and processed sugar, and feeling better than ever before.

How does food get to our plates? What is its origin? How was it treated? Are there additives? What are they? I have heard these questions with remarkable regularity. Conventional nutritional advice is being challenged because our western diets are leading to a nation of unhealthy people. An increase in food-related illnesses has made people less trusting of the traditional purveyors of food and less willing to accept the marketing claims made by packaged-food manufacturers.

Having said this, we all still want our food to *taste great*. Whether you are a sometime vegetarian or a new vegan or someone who's been eating this way for years, Ruth's and co-author Jennifer Houston's experience and expertise are at your disposal in this, the second Fresh by Juice for Life cookbook.

Little did I realize when I first saw Ruth that she was actually way out in front of a wave now entering the mainstream. In the years since, Ruth and Jennifer have enhanced and perfected the wonderful fare on offer at their various restaurant locations. Their signature dishes, many of which appear between these covers, borrow from global cuisine and meld common and uncommon ingredients in a provocative and tantalizing manner.

I know you will enjoy the wonderful tastes and healthy benefits that *Fresh at Home* proclaims.

## *Carlo Rota*

actor and host of *The Great Canadian Food Show*

# growing roots the fresh story

I remember a time, many years ago, when I vowed to make it on my own in the restaurant business, even if it took me twice as long. I would be free to make my own choices and mistakes with no interference or outside pressures. I've since discovered that behind every successful restaurateur is a level-headed chartered accountant (that's Barry Alper) and a hard-working executive chef (that's Jennifer Houston).

To achieve success, the small-business owner must be prepared to relinquish some control, be willing to delegate duties and chores and, most importantly, be able to recognize those things that might be better done by others. If the right people are in place, the result is regular days off, month-long winter holidays and perhaps even a published cookbook or two. Finding a balance between letting go and maintaining a strong presence has become my daily challenge.

I first met my business partner Barry Alper in April 1992. You see, my then boyfriend—who had introduced me to the joys of juicing, a healthy vegan diet and, ironically, a terribly unhealthy relationship—and I were splitting up and I had only ten days left to buy him out or lose the café. I needed a business plan quickly, and that's where Barry came in. One night, at the request of a mutual friend (Paul Bain, my customer and lawyer), Barry called me to offer his assistance. I gave Barry the details of my small business along with my hopes and dreams for the future and, in less than 24 hours, he gave me a business plan and a shot at achieving those goals. He never charged me a penny.

That same week my best friend, Rhonda Moscoe, was getting married up north. I couldn't let her down, so attended the wedding despite the fact I was panicking about my precarious business situation. A few glasses of wine into the reception, I got chatting with a New Yorker, the first cousin of the groom, and told him my whole crazy story. It turns out he was wealthy, sympathetic and willing to help. I sent him my business plan, and five days later, sight unseen, the money was in the bank and Juice for Life was safe in my hands. His name was Michael Bessen and he was an angel.

Over the next three years, Juice for Life grew into a thriving juice bar and vegan café in the Queen Street Market, across from Citytv. The juice bar/café was only 400 square feet with a 10 × 10 foot kitchen and an eating counter with just eight stools. Although I made the most of what I had to work with, I knew I could accomplish much more with a larger space.

Barry, who had continued to be a generous source of financial advice and moral support, became my business partner in 1995. He secured a loan from the bank that enabled me to purchase a much larger Hungarian schnitzel eatery on Bloor Street West, in the heart of Toronto's funky Annex area. With the help of many generous friends, we transformed the space into a 50-seat vegan restaurant and gourmet juice bar.

**Ruth and Barry**

At the start, I fretted that Barry, now part owner, wasn't a true vegetarian. As time passed, however, Barry's mainstream sensibilities proved to be a good balance for my somewhat more extreme mindset. Ironically, as Juice for Life's alternative roots inched toward the mainstream, Barry's eating habits inched closer to the alternative. That's the subversive outcome of eating delicious, wholesome, healthy food on a daily basis; it's hard to go back. For my part, I was thankful to have someone in my corner who believed in the concept and who had a vested interest in sticking it out through all the growing pains.

The spring of 1998 was a pivotal time for Juice for Life. Our original location, which had been closed for several months, reopened down the street in a bigger, better space. A week after we opened, our long-time head chef and her lover, the baker, suddenly disappeared with our entire book of recipes. Convinced they had the only set, the chef and the baker called a few days later from somewhere in the southwestern United States with a ransom request of $30,000 for the return of the recipes. We called their bluff and told them they were welcome to them. Incredibly, a week earlier I had awoken in the night feeling uneasy that we had only one copy of our recipes, many of which were handwritten. I dragged my husband, Rich, out of bed to get the book of recipes at the restaurant, and we photocopied all of them at Kinko's. Thank goodness! Months later we heard the ladies had settled down in Arizona and were managing a fast-food burger franchise.

The chef's unexpected departure opened the door for Jennifer Houston's arrival. Hired less than two weeks earlier, Jennifer had already begun to stand out as a talented cook with the right stuff to make it in our bustling kitchen of misfits. Amidst the unfolding drama,

**Jen at work**

Jennifer quickly took the helm as executive chef. As her confidence grew, the quality, consistency and presentation of the food served at both locations surpassed anything we had done so far. Soon Jennifer was improving upon existing recipes and creating a diverse array of specials and menu items, many of which are in this cookbook. It was a pleasant surprise to learn that Jennifer's superior qualities weren't limited to cooking. She was also flexible, organized, good natured, smart, well liked and respected by her staff.

It was clear to Barry and me that for Juice for Life to continue to grow, and before anyone else stole her away, we needed to secure Jennifer's future in the company. In 2000, Jennifer became a partner in Juice for Life. This smart decision eased much of the pressure on me to be everywhere at once each day.

By February 2002, Juice for Life had blossomed into Fresh. Fresh was a name chosen to reflect and recognize that we had now become more than just a great juice bar. Fresh food, fresh juice, fresh ingredients and fresh ideas had become our daily mantra.

We always said that if the day came that we were lined up every night, we'd know it was time to begin the search for a third location. (You know business is booming when the owners can't get a table at their own restaurant.) After several false starts in April 2002, we found a fantastic corner location with a west-facing patio in the city's west end. This time around we spent the money and time to "do it right" by hiring an architectural firm, Giannone Associates, to design the space. The end result is an organic, beautiful, modern and serene space with an open kitchen and gorgeous juice bar. Over the past year, this location has won several prestigious architectural and design awards.

As with our other locations, this one has turned out to be a high-profile spot, located at the corner of Queen West and Crawford Street in Toronto's downtown. West Queen West is known to many local urbanites as an up-and-coming neighbourhood filled with lofts, designers, galleries and trendy shops.

In the end, I'm not disappointed that I didn't make it all this way on my own as I set out to do 12 years ago. Although the essence remains the same, my vision for Juice for Life has grown beyond what I could have hoped for. I have many more Fresh dreams yet to fulfill and, I hope, longer exotic holidays to take.

Juicefully Yours,

*Ruth Tal Brown*

**Fresh on Bloor**

**Fresh on Queen**

**Fresh on Crawford**

# shaking the tree ruth and jen

## THREE WEEKS TO THE DEADLINE

Let me tell you, writing this book has been one of the most excruciating processes since my final set of exams in high school. And, if you've read the first cookbook, you know that high school did not end very well for me—because I never actually finished it. This book has been the ultimate test of my character. Unlike high school, where I was incredibly good at rationalizing my failures, I have had no choice but to stick with it and hand in this manuscript on time.

I thought it would be easier the second time around, but it has been quite the opposite. The first cookbook had been percolating inside my head and heart for nearly a decade; it poured out of me.

This time, I've had to reach deeper to find my direction, my voice and what it is I think you might like to know. This has proven to be a revealing process, forcing me to take stock of who I am in my business today, where I draw my inspiration from and what my hopes and dreams are for the future of Fresh. Are they the same as when I first started my business 12 years ago? Yes. True, I am no longer the 20-something young woman who created Juice for Life, wishing to evangelize the entire world, one by one, to the wonders of being vegan and treading gently on this precious planet of ours. At 38 I admit I am a little jaded and less idealistic, but nonetheless vegan, still inspired and hopeful. I love my work, and I still want to do my part in making a positive contribution to this world. This is how I do it.

Although compiling the recipes was much easier, thanks to co-author Jennifer Houston, the dream of taking six months off to write this cookbook like I did the last time was not to be. Jennifer and I have been in the trenches running the three Fresh restaurants during this entire writing process. The truth is, we live and breathe the recipes you are about to see.

Whereas in the first book I managed to maintain healthy eating habits through the entire writing process, this time I munched on potato chips, sweets and chocolate soy ice cream and drank gallons of ginger ale and hot chocolate. I surrendered to my vices to get me through the hours hunched in front of the computer screen. I did, however, manage to resist the temptation to fuel my writing with caffeine for fear of causing irreparable damage to my marriage!

As we near the conclusion, I see that this has been an enormous learning experience. I have

a huge sense of relief and satisfaction, like when you finally hand in that big assignment you struggled over and that you know was worthy of the time spent. So, I want to thank you for getting me to do this crazy thing called "writing a cookbook." I never dared to dream I would have this opportunity again.

I hope you enjoy it.
Peace,

*Ruth*

Three Days to the Deadline
I succumb to coffee.

## JEN'S STORY

Little did I know five years ago, when I walked into Fresh (then called Juice for Life) on Bloor Street in Toronto, that my life was about to change. The journey that led here began about three years before that, when I enrolled in cooking school. I was living in Kingston after graduating from university, with absolutely no idea what I wanted to do with my life. I worked in a pub, and one day we had to cater a function, so I was asked to help out in the kitchen. This was a defining moment. Never before had it occurred to me to cook for a living, even though all I did in my spare time was cook, watch cooking shows and read cookbooks. I probably flipped about 10,000 eggs working Sunday brunches at the pub, but it hooked me. Soon after, I moved to Toronto to attend George Brown College's hospitality program.

Throughout my training, I always felt that the regular chef route of working in hotels or "fine dining establishments" was not for me—yet I had no idea what kind of place was for me. After graduation (and still undecided as to where I would work), a friend and I decided to move to Britain. After a brief stay in London, we ended up in Edinburgh, Scotland, where I landed a job at Henderson's, a vegetarian restaurant that has been around since the 1960s.

In no time at all I decided to become vegetarian, which was one of the easiest decisions I ever made. (This decision coincided with the appearance of mad cow disease, an outbreak of E. coli that killed some senior citizens and a scandal involving disgruntled employees at a grocery store who mixed floor sweepings into the ground beef on sale.) Giving up meat led to a revelation: I had never really liked it anyway and was probably eating it only out of habit.

A year later I was back in Toronto, working at various cooking jobs until the day a friend saw an ad in the paper for the position of sous chef at Juice for Life. Two days later, I walked in for my first shift. Two weeks later, after the sudden departure of the head chef, I was in charge. This was not (as I'm sure you can imagine) an easy time. I still didn't really know the menu, the staff didn't know or trust me, and yet I was supposed to be leading the team. But, there was something about this place . . . I had a feeling that if I stuck it out, I could make a difference.

Four years later, Ruth and her business partner, Barry Alper, offered me a partnership in the restaurants. I am truly fortunate to work in an industry I love and to create food that challenges and excites me. And, of course, I'm very lucky to have business partners whom I respect and trust. Believe me, it would be torture to try to run three restaurants with people you didn't like and couldn't have a laugh with.

Although some people may think it is very limiting to make only vegan food, I find it the opposite. Over the years at Fresh, the thing that drives me, above all, is taste. I'm not prepared to eat something that has little or no flavour just because it's good for me, and neither should you. In my mind, eating vegan shouldn't be about sacrificing pleasure, and my hope is that once you have tried some of these recipes, you will agree.

As with all things, the kitchen at Fresh is constantly evolving. New ideas and recipes are being created daily. So it seemed only natural to do a second cookbook and to share our new favourites with you. We hope you enjoy using it as much as we have enjoyed writing it.

*Jennifer Houston*

# fresh at home

# fresh
## food recipes

**Our Wall of Fame**

# the fresh kitchen

For a little more than a decade, vegetarian eating has been at the heart of a culinary revolution in North America. The driving force behind this groundswell is a public increasingly aware of what they eat and how it affects their health. A health-conscious and sophisticated attitude now influences people's eating habits and choices. And, whereas in the past vegetarian dishes were often bland and boring, today vegetarian cuisine is typically light, vibrant, varied and creative.

Since our first vegetarian cookbook, *Juice for Life: Modern Food and Luscious Juice,* hit the stands three years ago, the menu at our restaurants—all called Fresh—has continued to expand and evolve. Fresh at Home is a response to the many requests we've received over the past few years for more Fresh recipes. Many of the recipes are popular menu items, while others are gathered from our enormous collection of daily evening and lunch specials.

Over the past three years we've created a range of exciting new dishes, many including ingredients such as aramé, hijiki, hulled hemp seeds, shiitake mushrooms and adzuki beans. In addition to their high nutritional value, these wonderful ingredients have added new layers of flavour and texture throughout the menu. We all need food to fuel our bodies, but good healthy food also feeds the soul. The food at Fresh is known to comfort and satisfy the urge for a home-cooked meal. Preparing these recipes in your own kitchen gives you the best of what we offer without having to leave your home.

Although these recipes call for no animal products, we can assure you that nothing here will leave you feeling deprived. Most people who are new to preparing this kind of cuisine may at first be intimidated by certain "mysterious" ingredients, but the truth is, these recipes are all remarkably simple and the ingredients easily attainable. Keep in mind that the following recipes have survived and succeeded in our busy kitchens precisely because training new cooks in a high-volume restaurant makes it essential that recipes be easy to grasp and quick to prepare.

## DIFFERENT STROKES

Knowing what is best for you and following through on it takes a certain amount of discipline—always a good thing. But there's a fine line between a healthy self-discipline and a neurotic approach to food choices. For those who have imposed a phalanx of rules and regulations dictating what, when and how to eat, the process of dining—whether in or out—can be fraught with stress.

Some dietary restrictions are imposed on us by our own bodies (through food allergies, sensitivities, etc.), while some are self-imposed. Whatever style of eating you choose for yourself—vegetarian, vegan, macrobiotic, raw, wheat- or gluten-free or a blend of several different styles—the key is to relax, savour the moment and enjoy your food.

The following is a list of dietary styles that have become increasingly common.

## VEGETARIAN

There are three kinds of vegetarians:

1. Lacto-vegetarians eat no animal products such as fish, meat, poultry or eggs but will include dairy products in their diet.
2. Ovo-vegetarians eat no animal or dairy products but will eat eggs.
3. Lacto-ovo vegetarians eat no animal products but will include dairy and eggs in their diet.

## VEGAN

A vegan diet is a style of eating that excludes *all* animal products including fish, meat, poultry and animal by-products such as eggs and dairy. This diet is based on a balanced intake of fruits, vegetables, legumes, grains, nuts, seeds, herbs, flowers and spices. Food may be raw, cooked or processed. Bee by-products, such as honey, bee pollen or royal jelly, are not considered vegan.

## MACROBIOTIC

The macrobiotic approach to food and life in general begins with the underlying belief that health lies in the fine balance of opposites; the balance between the mental and physical, plant and animal, cooked and raw, salt and oil, sweet and savoury, hot and cold, and our inner and outer worlds. Macrobiotic is the harmony and balance of the yin and the yang. Yin is considered passive and is traditionally associated with water, cold, the body, the feminine and dark. Yang, on the other hand, is considered active, with qualities including fire, heat, the mind, the masculine and light.

On the extreme yin side of foods are meat, poultry, eggs, hard dairy foods and refined salt. On the extreme yang side are soft dairy products, tropical fruits and vegetables, honey and sugar, coffee and other stimulants and alcohol. Between these two extremes lies the category of foods that macrobiotics embrace in their diet. The macrobiotic diet is built on whole grains, vegetables, beans, sea vegetables, tofu, fish, seeds, nuts and some fruit. Soups, brown rice, ginger and miso figure prominently in a macrobiotic diet. This style of eating is especially suited to cold winter climates due to the large amount of mostly warm cooked foods.

## RAW OR LIVING FOODS DIET

A raw diet (also known as a living foods diet) follows the principle that food must never be subjected to heat above 120°F. A raw or living foods diet excludes all animal products, including dairy and eggs. Living foods are fruits, vegetables, grains, beans, nuts, roots and seeds. Grains and beans are soaked and sprouted for eating and optimal nutrition. Virtually all edible plants that have not been cooked can be included in a raw diet. Subjecting fresh foods to heat causes precious enzymes and essential nutrients to be greatly diminished in value; they begin to die. That's why it's called a living foods diet. The undisputed benefits that result from eating raw foods include increased energy, mental alertness, a strong immune system, efficient digestion, clear skin and healthy hair. This style of nourishing your body is especially suited to spring, summer and fall climates, when an abundance of fresh and varied produce is available.

This cookbook is a resource for people who want to venture into vegetarianism but aren't sure how to get started. In addition to more than 125 vegetarian and vegan recipes, you'll find useful tips and techniques to help you get the best and most flavourful results. Refer to "Stocking Your Kitchen Cupboard" for helpful information on what to always have on hand and for in-depth information regarding such Fresh staples as tempeh, miso and soymilk, how tofu is actually made, why sprouts are good for you and how different sea vegetables such as aramé, nori and hijiki are harvested. Finally, we also include a glossary defining unusual ingredients.

Our fundamental guiding principle is to serve beautiful food that is delicious and healthy. Our focus lies in the positive aspects of a plant-based diet, avoiding dwelling on the negative aspects of eating meat. As we've found, this plant-based approach leaves you feeling energized, revitalized and deeply nourished—an added bonus and certainly no accident.

To great friends and family, staff, customers and readers alike, happy days and vibrant health.

*Ruth and Jennifer*

# kitchen tips

It's easy to prepare delicious food. All you need are high-quality ingredients, the right equipment, a knowledge of basic cooking techniques and some insider advice. The following kitchen tips and techniques will help you to get the best results.

## EQUIPPING YOUR KITCHEN

Here are the basic items you will need to make most of the recipes in this book:

- large heavy-bottomed saucepan
- large heavy-bottomed frying pan or wok
- blender or hand blender
- food processor
- chef's knife and paring knife
- spice or coffee grinder
- strainer or colander
- peeler
- cutting board
- box grater (if you don't have a food processor with a grating attachment)
- measuring spoons and cups

## GRINDING SPICES

The secret to getting good flavour in your recipes is to grind whole spices right before you use them. We use a mini coffee grinder just for grinding spices.

## CHILI POWDER

The chili powder we use in our recipes is also called "Mexican chili powder" and is a blend of various spices mixed with garlic powder. If you cannot purchase it, you can make your own:

| | | |
|---|---|---|
| **3 tbsp ground red chilies** | **1-1/2 tbsp garlic powder** | **1-1/2 tbsp ground oregano** |
| **1-1/2 tbsp ground cumin** | **1 tsp sea salt** | |

Mix together and store in an airtight container.

## REDUCING WINE

When cooking with wine, reduce the wine so that you are left with the flavour, not the alcohol. To do this, bring the wine to a boil and let at least half of it evaporate before adding other liquid ingredients.

## OILS

At the Fresh restaurants, we use many different kinds of oils: canola for grilling; sunflower for salad dressings; and olive for sautéing, salad dressings and many recipes. At home, you can make do with just sunflower and olive. Sunflower oil is light in flavour and colour, and is good for times when you need an oil that doesn't add any flavour. Olive oil is good in dressings and sauces, and for pan-frying. There are many different grades of olive oil, from the top-level extra virgin to the lowest grade, pomace. Extra virgin is from the first pressing after olives are harvested. Pomace is derived by squeezing out the olive pulp left over after making extra virgin and regular olive oil. For everyday home use, we recommend a mid-range regular olive oil—don't waste your money on an expensive extra-virgin for cooking because the flavour will be lost anyway. Good quality extra virgin olive oil should be saved for drizzling on salads, vegetables or bread—and anywhere that you can really appreciate its flavour.

## ROASTING PEPPERS

Roasting brings out the sweetness in red, yellow and orange bell peppers and creates a velvety texture. To roast peppers, place either on an open flame or on a hot burner. Turn the pepper as it cooks, until the skin is black. Place in a bowl and tightly cover with plastic wrap or a lid to trap the steam. Wait until the pepper is cool enough to handle, then remove the skin and seeds. Proceed with the recipe or slice and eat.

## PREPARING BEANS

In our recipes, we usually call for cup amounts of cooked beans (2 cups of cooked beans is the equivalent of one 19-ounce can).

If you are using dried beans and forgot to soak them overnight, use the following quick-soak method: Put the beans into a pot of water and bring to a boil. Remove from heat and let the beans sit for an hour before draining. This method will result in beans similar to those that have been soaked for eight hours.

## PREPARING RICE NOODLES

Often called "rice stick," these noodles are available dried in most health food stores, large supermarkets and Asian food stores. To use, separate the amount you need from the rest of the pack (you'll have to break them apart), put into a large bowl and cover with cold water. Let soften for about 30 minutes. Drain and proceed with the recipe. Note that rice stick still need to be cooked.

Rice stick come in various thicknesses, from thread-like vermicelli to about a quarter-inch wide. We like to use the largest ones in our noodles dishes. Soaked rice noodles can stay in the fridge for a couple of days.

## TOASTING NUTS AND SEEDS

To get more flavour from your nuts and seeds, toast them. You can do this two ways—either in a dry pan over medium heat, or on a cookie tray in a 350°F oven. Either way takes only about three to five minutes, so don't walk away, as nuts and seeds tend to go from raw to burnt in the blink of an eye.

## PURÉEING

At the Fresh restaurants, we purée our soups using a large commercial hand immersion blender. This means that we can purée soups while they are still hot. If you don't have a hand blender and want to use a regular blender, cool any hot liquid before you blend it. No matter how tightly you put the lid on your blender, if the liquid is hot it will explode right out of the blender, sending the lid and the contents all over your kitchen, and worse, all over you!

## SAUTÉING

The original meaning of the word "sauté" is to jump, or to toss things in a pan over heat. Now, sauté is widely used to mean pan-fry. To pan-fry without burning, use medium heat and a heavy-bottomed skillet.

## EMULSIFYING

Emulsification is the process used to make traditional mayonnaise and hollandaise sauces or dressings. An emulsification is a suspension of one liquid within another liquid, usually oil; in other words, bringing two thin ingredients, such as oil and vinegar, together to create one thick liquid. This can be achieved by hand with a bowl and whisk, or by mechanical means with a blender or food processor.

For an emulsion to occur, add the oil very slowly so that each molecule of oil gets attached to a molecule of the other ingredients. Sometimes, if you add the oil too quickly, your dressing will break, meaning the ingredients will separate, and resist thickening. If this happens, take most of the dressing out of the blender, leaving about 1/4 cup. Very slowly, in a thin stream, with the blender running, add the broken dressing. Usually this will re-emulsify the dressing.

## ZESTING

Zesting means thinly peeling or grating the rind of a citrus fruit, excluding the white fibre called the pith. The thin rind, also known as zest, is commonly grated for use in baking. Although a box or cheese grater will do, a zester—the tool solely designed to grate citrus rind—is available in all kitchen stores.

## STOCKING YOUR KITCHEN CUPBOARD

We encourage you to get acquainted with these wonderful ingredients. Welcome them into your kitchen, and they will quickly become favourite staples. You'll soon wonder how you ever managed without them.

When buying herbs and spices, it is much cheaper to go to a bulk food store to buy small quantities rather than pay for those astronomically priced bottles in the supermarket.

## SAUCES AND OILS

| | | |
|---|---|---|
| apple cider vinegar | olive oil | tahini (sesame butter) |
| balsamic vinegar | rice vinegar | tamari |
| Bragg's liquid aminos | sambal oelek | toasted sesame oil |
| miso (light) | sunflower oil | |

## SEASONINGS

| | | |
|---|---|---|
| black pepper | Dijon mustard | fresh ginger |
| curry powder | fresh garlic | sea salt |

## HERBS AND SPICES

| | | |
|---|---|---|
| anise | cumin | paprika |
| basil | dill | red chili flakes |
| cayenne pepper | garlic powder | rosemary |
| chili powder | marjoram | sage |
| cinnamon | nutmeg | thyme |
| coriander | oregano | |

## NOODLES AND RICE

| | | |
|---|---|---|
| brown basmati rice | rice noodles | soba noodles |

## NUTS AND SEEDS

| | | |
|---|---|---|
| almonds | hulled hemp seeds | sesame seeds |
| cashews | pumpkin seeds | sunflower seeds |

## LEGUMES

| | | |
|---|---|---|
| adzuki beans | chickpeas | split peas (yellow and green) |
| black beans | lentils (red, green) | |

## OTHER

| | | |
|---|---|---|
| aramé | nutritional yeast | raw, unrefined sugar |
| coconut milk | pure maple syrup | |

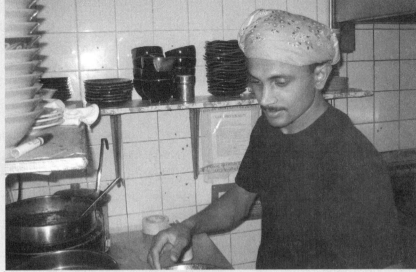

Jeya, head receiver (top)

Laura and Courtney on the line (bottom)

# FRESH FACTS

## TOFU

The Chinese have prepared and consumed bean curd since 200 B.C. In North America, tofu—the Japanese name for bean curd—has become a major source of easily digestible protein in most vegetarian and vegan diets since the 1960s. Today, tofu enjoys a growing, if sometimes begrudging, acceptance as a necessary food because of its nutritious profile.

Among its nutrients, tofu contains B-vitamins, calcium, phosphorous, iron, sodium and potassium. It has only 18 calories per ounce. At Fresh, tofu is a prominent element in our cuisine because of its versatility. Used in sweet or savoury dishes, tofu can be steamed, baked, fried, broiled, grilled or eaten raw. (To keep tofu from drying out, cover it with water in an airtight container and refrigerate. Change the water every other day.)

Unless otherwise specified, our recipes call for firm tofu, which contains less water, is more versatile and is much easier to work with. The more tofu is drained, the more flavour it absorbs.

We cut tofu into cubes or triangles and then marinate (page 132) before using. Crispy Tofu Coating (page 130) is especially popular at Fresh.

Japanese-style tofu is made with a precipitating agent or coagulant called nigari, a sea salt extract, which provides flavour. Chinese-style tofu is made with a different coagulant, calcium chloride, which we think doesn't taste as good but is higher in calcium.

## MAKING TOFU

1. Soybeans are soaked for 12 to 15 hours.
2. They are drained, rinsed and ground in a bean grinder with triple-filtered water. This mixture is known as "slurry."
3. The slurry is pumped into a very large steam or pressure cooker and cooked at a high temperature for about 5 minutes.
4. The cooked slurry is cooled to below the boiling point and spun in a centrifuge to separate the milk from the pulp, also known by its Japanese name, okara. The milk is pumped into a separate tank; okara is used mainly to feed livestock.

5. The soymilk is then poured into curdling barrels and a precipitating agent is added, which causes curds to form. The curds are then stirred by hand or by machines for 30 to 40 minutes.

6. The whey, which is the liquid left over after the protein has formed into curds, is drained off and discarded. The remaining curds are removed and placed into boxes lined with cheesecloth to form into large blocks of tofu.

7. The large blocks are then cut into smaller blocks, placed in filtered water and chilled. They are now ready for packaging.

## TEMPEH

Tempeh (pronounced tem-pay) is a fermented high-protein product made from whole soybeans, created in Indonesia and traditionally used in Thai, Indonesian and Malaysian cooking. To make tempeh, whole soybeans are soaked in water, hulled, boiled, formed into cakes or patties and left to ferment. Fermentation makes digestion of the soy protein easier. Tempeh is often confused with tofu; however, they are actually very different in appearance, texture and taste. In fact, tofu, smooth, silky and neutral in flavour, is produced from the curds of fermented soymilk, while tempeh is meaty, chewy and nutty in flavour and produced from the whole soybean. Unlike other fermented soy products, such as tofu or soy sauce, tempeh does not contain salt. There are up to 30 varieties of tempeh available; different kinds are made by combining soybeans with other ingredients such as brown rice, millet, quinoa, sea vegetables or sesame seeds and allowing the mixture to ferment for varying lengths of time.

Tempeh makes an excellent substitute for meat, poultry or fish. It is also an excellent source of vitamin B12—a bonus for vegans. The tempeh found in most natural food stores is frozen, but it comes fresh, dried or precooked. Although fresh tempeh is tastier, it is also highly perishable, which is why we buy ours frozen. You can either thaw it at room temperature or briefly blanch it before cooking.

Eaten raw, tempeh is difficult for the body to digest, potentially creating gas and discomfort. Although it can be steamed, baked, fried, broiled or grilled, we prefer to slice our tempeh into thin strips, marinate (page 131) and grill. Grilled tempeh appears in Revival Rice Bowl (page 62), Satori Noodles (page 82) and BBQ Tempeh Wrap (page 89).

## SOY SAUCE AND TAMARI

Soy sauce is a fermented dark brown salty liquid made from soybeans, wheat, salt, alcohol and water. It is the chief savoury seasoning ingredient in Asian cooking but is becoming increasingly popular around the world. Ordinary soy contains 40 percent to 60 percent more wheat than tamari, which is the Cadillac of soy sauces. Popular in Southeast Asia, it is a naturally brewed soy sauce without preservatives or MSG. It is brewed with a lower proportion of wheat and salt, and therefore has less alcohol than regular soy sauce, and with more soybeans, so it contains 37 percent more soy protein than regular soy sauce. This higher concentration of soybeans causes tamari to ferment differently, meaning it retains its composition and richer, smooth flavour when heated. Since it doesn't break down or "flash" when exposed to high temperatures, it never gives food an overwhelmingly salty taste, instead heightening and enhancing the flavours of other ingredients. Use tamari in place of salt wherever possible to reduce sodium intake.

Tamari comes in organic, wheat free or low sodium. San-J makes an organic line of tamari sauce available in both wheat free and low sodium.

## MISO

Miso is a fermented soybean paste thought to have originated in China 2500 years ago. Miso consists of cooked soybeans, salt and various grains (barley or rice) that are fermented from two weeks to more than two years. Miso varieties differ in formulation, salt concentration and fermenting time. Miso ranges in flavour and texture from sweet and delicate to meaty and savoury. The darker varieties, reds and browns, tend to be riper, higher in salt and stronger in flavour. The lighter varieties, yellows and golds, are sweet and mild.

Miso is considered a living food that contains the same friendly bacteria found in yogurt, as well as traces of vitamin B12 and high levels of protein. The intense flavour that miso brings to any dish reduces the need to season with the usual fats, oils and salts. Boiling will kill the enzymes and nutrients in miso that make it good for you, so add miso only after a pot comes off the heat. This will also ensure that the miso flavour isn't overly concentrated and intense, as it would be if boiled for any length of time. Miso keeps better if stored in glass (rather than plastic) in a cool place.

## SOYMILK

Have you ever wondered why "soymilk" is written as one word? Speculation is that writing soymilk as one word coined a phrase rather than identified it as a proper "milk," so as to remain outside the heavily regulated area of dairy products.

Soymilk is a relative newcomer to the scene compared with other traditional soy products such as tofu, miso and tempeh. In China, soymilk production was a small traditional cottage industry because soymilk was never a predominant element in people's diets. The first patent for soymilk was issued to Li Yu-ying, in 1910, in France. This marked the introduction in Europe of the concept of milk made from something other than cows, goats or sheep. The rising popularity of soymilk and related soy products has sparked a lively competition between the young soymilk industry and the giant dairy industry in Europe and North America.

Strictly speaking, soymilk is a water extract of whole soybeans. Commercial soymilks today are sweetened and also contain added oil and salt. There are several kinds of soymilk commonly available at stores these days: original (plain), vanilla, chocolate, vitamin enriched and low fat. A growing number of people are turning to other non-dairy alternatives as well, such as rice milk, almond milk and oat milk. Soymilk, however, is the closest to dairy milk in consistency and texture and is the best choice for cooking or baking. At Fresh, we prefer to use an organic original (plain) soymilk, which is less sweet, for our cooking recipes. At the juice bar we use organic vanilla soymilk for our Power Shakes, Pro Athletic Shakes (page 192) and Lassis (page 198). Creamy vanilla soymilk also makes good foam for hot chai, cappuccinos and lattes. Other non-dairy alternatives tend to be lower in fat and therefore do not foam as well for espresso drinks.

## SPROUTS

Sprouts remind us of happy things like spring, growth, fresh air, sunny days and new beginnings. Sprouting is the germination of raw nuts, seeds, grains and legumes by soaking them in water and giving them time to grow. Sprouts represent the point of greatest vitality in the life cycle of a plant; vitamins, minerals, proteins and essential fatty acids that lie dormant are activated and then multiply rapidly in the first five to seven days. A wide variety of beans, grains and seeds can be sprouted, such as sunflower seeds, pumpkin seeds, fenugreek seeds, buckwheat, lentils, chickpeas, wheat berries, broccoli, alfalfa and many more. Super Sprouts, a wonderful sprouting operation in Toronto, grows all our organic sprouts as well as supplies us with fresh-cut wheat grass for juicing.

Sprouts are easy to assimilate and require far less energy to digest than other foods. Sprouting removes certain acids and toxins found in plant life that can interfere with digestion. Grains and legumes, many of which are common allergens, often do not cause allergies when sprouted. For example, most people with wheat allergies can drink wheat grass juice with no negative reaction, and people who don't digest regular beans very well have no problem eating sprouted beans.

At the Fresh restaurants we use a variety of sprouts—sunflower sprouts, buckwheat sprouts, alfalfa sprouts, pea green sprouts and bean sprouts—in our salads, sandwiches, wraps, rice bowls, noodle dishes and appetizers. Each has its own unique taste and appearance. The sunflower sprout is our favourite sprout for taste while the pea green sprout is our first choice for dramatic appearance in a dish. Buckwheat sprouts are delicious and have pretty pink stems. We like to use alfalfa sprouts in sandwiches for their volume, taste and texture. Other fabulous sprouts for food preparation are radish, broccoli, lentil, chickpea, fenugreek, peanut and adzuki bean sprouts. The produce sections of supermarkets, high-end grocery stores and natural food stores usually have a good selection.

## SEA VEGETABLES

Sea vegetables, such as hijiki, aramé, nori, kombu and dulse contain 10 to 20 times the minerals of land plants. Often referred to as seaweeds, sea vegetables come in different colours, ranging from greens to reds and browns. The colour is affected by the amount of sunlight available underwater to the plant for photosynthesis. Light exposure, depth and temperature create different environments that correspond to the distribution of nutrients among sea plants. The more light available to the plant, the greener the plant, and therefore the more nutrients present in the plant.

At Fresh, we marinate hijiki and aramé (see Marinated Aramé and Hijiki, page 134) before adding them to a variety of salads, rice bowls and noodle dishes. Both hijiki and aramé are high in sodium because they come from the sea, and they should be eaten in moderation by anyone on a low-sodium diet.

## HIJIKI

Hijiki (hi-she-kee) has brown tendrils that grow over rocks in the sea. The harvested plants are cut, dried in the sun, boiled until soft and dried again until they are black. Hijiki has a nutty aroma and distinct sea flavour. Marinating and cooking it with other ingredients will reduce the fishy flavour if you find it too strong. The thick rope-like strips, which expand to twice their volume when soaked, give a whole new texture to a dish. Hijiki is an excellent source of calcium, iron and iodine. Available at most natural food stores, hijiki is the most costly of the sea vegetables. It must be soaked for 5 to 15 minutes before it is ready for marinating (see Marinated Aramé and Hijiki, page 134) and food preparation.

Hijiki is included in the Tsunami Noodles (page 78) and the Hijiki Rice Bowl (page 68).

## ARAMÉ

Aramé (ar-a-may) has a dark yellow-brown colour. It grows in bunches intertwined with other sea vegetables. This sea vegetable is very tough and is chopped into string-like strips, then boiled and dried in the sun to a charcoal black. Aramé's mild sweet flavour makes it the most versatile of all the sea vegetables. We use it most often as a topping for our salads and rice bowls. Aramé is one of the richest sources of iodine. It also has highly concentrated doses of iron and calcium.

Like hijiki, aramé must be soaked first for 5 to 15 minutes before marinating (see Marinated Aramé and Hijiki, page 134) and food preparation. Aramé appears in The Raw Truth Salad (page 38), Green Destiny Salad (page 39), Love Nest (page 46), Revival Rice Bowl (page 62) and the Tantric Rice Bowl (page 65).

## NORI

Nori, which is a jade-green colour, is harvested in Japan, Ireland and Scotland. Once harvested, it is dried and pressed flat into paper-thin sheets and toasted. The fibres of nori are more tender and delicate than other sea vegetables: its tasty and delicate flavour explains why it is the preferred wrap for sushi rolls or is torn and added to soups and rice bowls. Rich in vitamins A, B1 and niacin, nori has the highest protein content and is most easily digested of all the sea vegetables.

At Fresh, nori is added to the Gospel Rice Bowl (page 71) and to the Supreme Udon Noodles (page 83).

## GRAINS

Ancestors of the whole wheat family, including spelt, buckwheat, kamut, amaranth and quinoa, are low in gluten and are better tolerated by people who have difficulty in digesting wheat products. These ancient grains were originally farmed in the Middle or Near East as far back as 9000 years ago. People with wheat and gluten allergies do not generally react to spelt or the other ancient grains. Many nutritionists and naturopaths believe that the increasing sensitivity to wheat among the population is because, over the course of history, wheat has been hybridized and modified so much that it is no longer as nature intended. A growing awareness of the negative effects of even the mildest wheat and gluten sensitivities has caused people to seek alternative grain foods.

At Fresh, we tend to use spelt the most in our cooking and baking because it is closest to wheat in versatility without causing negative reactions. The spelt berry has a thick husk that protects it from pollutants and insects. It is a hearty grain with a delicate nutty taste and is higher in protein, fat and fibre than most varieties of wheat.

## YEAST

The three types of yeast we use at Fresh are active dry, nutritional and Engevita. Active dry yeast is used only in our pizza dough and breads. This yeast is a live plant that multiplies under certain conditions, creating carbon dioxide that in time produces light and airy baked goods. Nutritional yeast, often referred to by its commercial name Red Star, is grown on mineral-enriched molasses and is one of the rare vegetarian sources of vitamin

B12. Engevita yeast is a completely inactive yeast product derived from baker's yeast that is rich in amino acids, minerals and B-vitamins.

Both nutritional yeast and Engevita are food yeasts that can be used for many different applications such as gravies, sauces, seasonings, spice mixes and condiments. Their strong, savoury, nutty, almost cheese-like flavour is often the ingredient that makes all the difference in a recipe. In this cookbook, we use these yeasts in the Crispy Tofu Coating (page 130), Tofu Omelette (page 152) and Scrambled Tofu (page 138).

## HEMP

Hemp is a distinct variety of the plant species *cannabis sativa L.* The hemp plant is tall, slender and fibrous, similar to flax, and can grow to 14 feet. Civilizations throughout history—including those in India, Babylonia, Persia, Egypt and South America, and native cultures of North America and Europe—have cultivated the hemp plant. Recently, the United Nations legally recognized hemp as a commercial crop. (Actor Woody Harrelson, among others, has been a leading advocate for the economical and ecological benefits of using hemp for food and fibre in the United States.)

Hemp seeds contain no THC, the chemical in marijuana that makes you high. Hemp contains 34.6 percent protein, 46.5 percent fat, 11.6 percent carbohydrate and Omega 6 and Omega 3, both essential fatty acids. All essential amino acids can also be found in hemp. The protective shells of the hemp seeds are edible but tough and tend to get stuck between the teeth. Hulled hemp seeds, also referred to as hemp nut, are soft and have a pleasant nutty taste that is delicious in salads, rice bowls and smoothies. At Fresh, we include hulled hemp seeds in the Big Salad (page 41), the Revival Rice Bowl (page 62), the Hemp Lassi (page 200) and in the In the Raw elixir (page 182).

Other wonderful hemp products include cold-pressed hemp seed oil, hemp seed flour and hemp nut butter. Hemp oil, flour and butter have been used increasingly as main ingredients to make hemp beer, pasta, cheese, cookies, waffles, breads, granola and ice cream, most of which can be found in natural and health food stores. For leading brands of hemp products, look for Ruth's Hemp and Hempola products.

Soups are part of every culture, so in this section you'll find soups that draw inspiration from all over the world. Though soups are often thought of as appetizers, our soups can be described as a cozy meal in a bowl and range from rustic and chunky to smooth and velvety.

Soups can be adapted to the seasons and your moods by changing the thickness and texture. Even when you are working from a recipe you still have leeway to make your own adjustments. Prefer a thick and hearty soup? Cook it longer. Or a light and thin soup? Add more broth. Add a side salad and a chunk of multi-grain bread and you've created a nourishing and satisfying meal. Garnishes, where listed, are not meant as afterthoughts but rather are an integral part of the flavour and design of the dish.

When making soup, good ingredients are essential, none more so than a good vegetable stock. Though it is fine to use ready-made stocks, none can parallel a homemade stock. Keep in mind that store-bought vegetable stock powder is often saltier than homemade stock, so we recommend that you add sea salt at the very end according to your taste. Also, many store-bought stocks contain MSG, so read the label carefully. There are a few good stock powders out there that are found mostly at natural and health food stores.

Our soups last from a few days to a week in the fridge and also freeze well. The nice thing about soups is that they make great leftovers and taste even better for the next day or two. Make a batch on Sunday and get ahead on your cooking for the rest of the week.

Choose a big pot so you can stir without the soup overflowing. The heavy bottom on a good pot prevents the vegetables from scorching, so you can sauté right in the pot. We recommend using filtered or bottled water for stock or soup. Tap water, especially hot water, picks up residue in pipes and doesn't taste as good as filtered or bottled water. Cook soup at a steady simmer, not a rolling boil, and leave partially uncovered to let the steam escape so the soup thickens properly.

# soups

# roasted vegetable stock

This vegetable stock is simple to prepare. Roasting veggies before making them into stock gives a much richer flavour to the finished stock. This recipe is for a totally fat-free stock, but if you wanted, you could add some oil to the veggies while they are roasting, as this helps them to caramelize a bit better. This stock keeps in the fridge for up to a week or may be frozen.

**2 carrots, roughly chopped**

**3 celery stalks, roughly chopped**

**1 onion, roughly chopped**

**2 tomatoes, cored, roughly chopped**

**4 cloves garlic**

**2 cups mushrooms**

**16 cups filtered water**

**1/2 cup parsley, roughly chopped**

**1/2 tsp black peppercorns**

1. Put carrots, celery, onion, tomato, garlic and mushrooms on a baking sheet and pour approximately 1/4 cup water over vegetables.
2. Roast at 400°F for approximately 20 minutes or until vegetables start to brown at the edges.
3. Remove vegetables from the baking sheet and place in a large pot. Add the remaining water, parsley and black peppercorns.
4. Bring to a boil over high heat. Reduce heat and let simmer for about 2 hours.
5. Strain stock and chill.

MAKES 8 CUPS

# golden curried dal

Lentils, one of the world's oldest foods, come in many colours and sizes. This recipe calls for small red lentils (lal masoor dal) but you can also use small yellow lentils (moong dal) or white lentils (urad dal) or a combination of the three. Lentils are easy to digest and are low in calories and high in protein and fibre. Basmati rice accompanied by thick curried dal is a staple food for millions of vegetarians living in India. Our dal can be enjoyed as a hearty soup on its own, perhaps with a side of warm pita, or poured over brown rice. Spinach, tomato, sautéed mushrooms or eggplant may be added to dal for a complete meal in a bowl.

The taste of this soup depends largely on the curry powder that you use. At the restaurant, we like to use an Indian curry powder called Lalah's. It has lots of flavour and the perfect amount of heat. Curry powders are a blend of many different spices including ground coriander, cumin seeds, curry leaves, fenugreek, mustard seed, cinnamon, cloves, peppercorn, tamarind, chilies, cayenne and turmeric. Watch out for curries with too much turmeric, which makes them bitter and a very bright yellow. Turmeric should be one of the last ingredients listed on the package. Store spice mixtures in tightly sealed containers to preserve flavours.

Dal keeps for a day or two in the fridge and also freezes well. Once refrigerated, it tends to solidify, so just add a little bit of filtered water when you reheat it.

| | |
|---|---|
| 4 tbsp canola oil | 1/2 tsp turmeric |
| 2 cooking onions, diced | 2-1/2 cups red lentils |
| 1 carrot, peeled and diced | 8 cups Roasted Vegetable Stock (page 22) |
| 4 cloves garlic, minced | 1-3/4 cups coconut milk |
| 3 tbsp minced fresh ginger | 2 green onions, finely sliced |
| 2 tsp curry powder | 1/4 cup chopped cilantro |
| 1 tsp cumin, ground | |

1. Heat oil in a large pot over medium heat.
2. Stir in onions, carrot, garlic and ginger. Cook for 5 minutes or until onions are softened.
3. Stir in curry powder, cumin and turmeric; cook for 30 seconds.
4. Add lentils, Roasted Vegetable Stock and coconut milk.
5. Simmer for 20 minutes or until lentils are soft. Remove from heat.
6. Garnish with green onions and cilantro and serve.

SERVES 4–6

# sicilian white bean and tomato soup

These ingredients are used in abundance in Sicily. This soup takes no time at all to put together, yet it is very impressive when it's done. The potatoes provide an almost creamy quality that is unusual in a tomato-based soup.

3 tbsp olive oil

1 cooking onion, diced

4 cloves garlic, minced

1/2 cup red wine

5 tbsp tomato paste

1/4 batch Pesto (page 127)

2 potatoes, peeled and diced

4 cups crushed tomatoes

8 cups Roasted Vegetable Stock (page 22)

2 cups cooked white kidney beans (or canned)

6 cups chopped fresh spinach (packed tightly)

1. Heat oil in a large pot over medium heat.
2. Stir in onion and garlic. Cook for 5 minutes or until onion is softened.
3. Add red wine, and cook 1 to 2 minutes or until liquid is reduced by half.
4. Stir in tomato paste, Pesto, potatoes, crushed tomatoes and Roasted Vegetable Stock. Bring to a boil, reduce heat and simmer for 15 minutes or until potatoes are tender.
5. Add beans, and cook for 5 minutes until heated through.
6. Remove from heat. Stir in chopped fresh spinach and serve.

SERVES 4–6

# french mushroom soup

This soup is very rich and hearty. Serve with a side of thickly sliced multi-grain bread or sourdough baguette.

Porcini mushrooms are most easily found in their dried form. When you go to buy the porcinis, you might be put off by their cost. But they go a long way and they're worth it. You could make this soup without them, but it won't be quite as rich and flavourful.

| | |
|---|---|
| 1 cup filtered water | 1 tsp allspice |
| 1/4 cup dried porcini mushrooms | 1/2 tsp dried basil |
| 4 tbsp olive oil | 1/2 tsp dried marjoram |
| 1 cooking onion, diced | 2-1/2 tsp Cajun seasoning |
| 4 cloves garlic, minced | 8 cups sliced button OR cremini mushrooms |
| 1 stalk celery, diced | 2 tomatoes, cored and chopped |
| 1 medium carrot, peeled and diced | 5 cups Roasted Vegetable Stock (page 22) |
| 1/2 cup red wine | |

1. Bring water to a boil in a small pot, drop dried porcini mushrooms in, and remove from heat. Let soak until soft, about 10 minutes. Strain mushrooms, saving the liquid. If there is any sediment in the liquid, let it settle and then pour liquid off the top, or pour the liquid through a piece of cheesecloth or kitchen towel.
2. Heat oil in a large pot over medium heat.
3. Stir in onion, garlic, celery and carrot. Cook for 5 minutes or until slightly browned.
4. Add red wine, allspice, basil, marjoram and Cajun seasoning. Bring to a boil and simmer 1 to 2 minutes or until liquid is reduced by half.
5. Add remaining mushrooms, tomatoes and Roasted Vegetable Stock; bring to a boil. Reduce heat and simmer for about 15 minutes until mushrooms and tomatoes are very soft. Remove from heat.
6. Pour half the soup into a large bowl. Using a hand blender, blend until smooth, then pour back into the pot and mix. (If you are using a blender, let the soup cool before blending, then reheat.) Serve.

SERVES 4–6

# moroccan chickpea and stars soup

This soup was inspired by the Chicken and Stars soup that Jennifer's mum used to give her when she was a kid, home from school with a cold. Of course, the Moroccan accents in this soup come from Ruth's mom. There is something so satisfying and hearty about this soup, yet it is still light enough to enjoy in the middle of summer. And it's good for you too! Chickpeas and white kidney beans are high in fibre and are a good source of vitamins and minerals.

2 tbsp olive oil

2 cooking onions, diced

3 tbsp minced fresh ginger

2 cloves garlic, minced

Pinch ground cinnamon

Pinch allspice

Pinch ground coriander

Pinch ground cardamom (optional)

Pinch turmeric

Pinch cayenne pepper

1 tomato, cored and chopped

1/2 cup red lentils

8 cups Roasted Vegetable Stock (page 22)

1 cup cooked or canned chickpeas

1 cup white kidney beans, cooked (or canned)

1/2 cup pasta shapes (stars, alphabets or orzo)

1 tsp sea salt

1/4 tsp black pepper

1 tbsp lemon juice

1. Heat oil in a pot over medium heat.
2. Stir in onions, ginger and garlic. Cook for 5 minutes or until onions are softened.
3. Add cinnamon, allspice, coriander, cardamom, turmeric and cayenne pepper; cook for 2 minutes.
4. Stir in tomato, lentils and Roasted Vegetable Stock. Cook for 15 minutes or until lentils are softened.
5. Add chickpeas, beans and pasta. Cook until pasta is done, about 5 minutes.
6. Remove from heat. Stir in salt, black pepper and lemon juice. Serve.

SERVES 4–6

# thai carrot soup

Everyone loves the velvety texture and exotic flavour of this soup. It is very quick and simple to make. Cilantro, finely chopped red pepper, chopped peanuts, diced tofu or green onions are all wonderful garnishes for this soup.

You will get more juice from your limes and lemons if you first roll them on the counter while pressing on them.

2 tbsp olive oil

2 cooking onions, chopped

1 stalk celery, chopped

3 cloves garlic, minced

4 tbsp minced fresh ginger

4 tsp curry powder

6 cups Roasted Vegetable Stock
(page 22)

3 large carrots, peeled and chopped

1-3/4 cups coconut milk

1 lime, juiced

1 lemon, juiced

2 tsp sea salt

Pinch white pepper

1. Heat oil in a pot over medium heat.
2. Add onions, celery, garlic and ginger. Cook for 5 minutes or until onions are softened.
3. Add curry powder, and cook for 1 minute, stirring continuously.
4. Stir in Roasted Vegetable Stock and carrots. Cook for 15 minutes or until carrots are softened.
5. Add coconut milk and bring to a boil.
6. Remove from heat. Add lemon and lime juice.
7. Using a hand blender, blend until smooth. (If you are using a blender, let the soup cool before blending, then reheat.)
8. Add salt and white pepper. Serve.

SERVES 4–6

# tibetan lentil soup

This recipe makes a very thick soup. If you like it thinner, add more vegetable stock. Lentils are high in fibre and are a good source of protein and B-vitamins. They are also high in iron, zinc and calcium. The iron in lentils is most easily absorbed by the body when eaten with a source of vitamin C, such as green leafy vegetables.

Always sort through your lentils before using, because there are often little stones mixed in. Apparently, lentil merchants do this on purpose to increase the weight of the bags. A good way to sort your lentils is to put them on a cookie sheet, all at one end, and then, as you sort them, push them to the other end. It's worth the effort to avoid biting down on a stone.

5 tbsp olive oil

2 cooking onions, diced

3 cloves garlic, minced

2 small carrots, peeled and diced

2 stalks celery, chopped

Pinch cayenne pepper

2 tsp ground coriander

1-1/2 tsp ground cumin

2 tsp turmeric

2 potatoes, peeled and diced

2 cups green lentils

11 cups Roasted Vegetable Stock (page 22)

1/2 cup chopped cilantro

Pinch sea salt

1 lemon, cut into wedges

1. Heat oil in a pot over medium heat.
2. Add onions, garlic, carrots and celery. Cook for 5 minutes or until onions are softened.
3. Stir in cayenne pepper, coriander, cumin and turmeric; cook for a couple of minutes.
4. Add potatoes, lentils and Roasted Vegetable Stock. Cook for 15 minutes or until lentils are soft.
5. Remove from heat. Add cilantro and salt to taste.
6. Garnish with lemon and serve.

SERVES 4–6

# jamaican spinach soup

This velvety soup is a brilliant green that is very appealing, especially when garnished with finely sliced red pepper. If you like your food very spicy, increase the cayenne to taste.

You will notice that the spinach is added after the soup comes off the heat. Spinach barely needs to cook, so the heat left in the soup will be sufficient to soften it.

Spinach is high in antioxidants such as beta carotene and lutein, which helps lower blood cholesterol. It also has carbohydrates, protein, fibre, vitamins A and C, calcium, iron and folic acid. Zucchini is high in folic acid and potassium.

| | |
|---|---|
| 3 tbsp olive oil | 1/4 tsp allspice |
| 1 cooking onion, chopped | 1/4 tsp nutmeg |
| 2 stalks celery, chopped | 2 potatoes, peeled and diced |
| 4 cloves garlic, minced | 4 cups chopped zucchini |
| 2 tbsp minced fresh ginger | 6 cups Roasted Vegetable Stock (page 22) |
| 1 tbsp raw unrefined sugar | Pinch cayenne pepper |
| 2 tsp sea salt | 1 cup chopped fresh spinach (packed tightly) |
| 1/4 tsp turmeric | 1/2 red pepper, minced |

1. Heat oil in a pot over medium heat.
2. Add onion, celery, garlic, ginger and sugar. Cook for 5 minutes or until onion is softened.
3. Stir in salt, turmeric, allspice and nutmeg. Cook for a couple of minutes.
4. Add potatoes, zucchini and Roasted Vegetable Stock. Bring to a boil, reduce heat and simmer 10 minutes or until potatoes are soft.
5. Remove from heat. Add cayenne pepper and spinach.
6. Using a hand blender, blend until smooth. (If you are using a blender, let the soup cool before blending, then reheat.)
7. Garnish with minced red pepper and serve.

SERVES 4–6

# curried lentil with sage soup

This soup is based on a casserole served at Henderson's Vegetarian Restaurant in Edinburgh, Scotland. At Henderson's, it was a layered dish with lentil, bean and tomato stew on the bottom, and potatoes, zucchini and cheese on top. It was called Lentil and Butterbean Bake. The combination of curry and sage is unusual, but it works.

Our version comes out quite thick, so you can add water or stock if you prefer a thinner soup.

2 tbsp olive oil

1 cooking onion, diced

1 potato, peeled and diced

1 clove garlic, minced

2 cups zucchini, diced

1 tbsp curry powder

1 tsp dried sage

1 cup dried baby lima beans, soaked overnight and drained

2 cups red lentils

6 cups Roasted Vegetable Stock (page 22)

2 tsp tomato paste

3 cups canned crushed tomatoes

3/4 tsp sea salt

1.  Heat oil in a pot over medium heat.
2.  Add onion and potato; cook for 5 minutes or until onion is softened.
3.  Stir in garlic, zucchini, curry powder and sage. Cook for 1 minute.
4.  Add beans, lentils, Roasted Vegetable Stock, tomato paste and crushed tomatoes.
5.  Bring to a boil then simmer for at least 30 minutes or until lentils and beans are cooked. Add more water, if necessary, to allow beans to fully cook.
6.  Remove from heat. Add salt and serve.

SERVES 4–6

# east african pea soup

We love this soup, which reminds us of faraway exotic places. The flavour here is savoury, with a little bit of sweetness from the sweet potato. Ten cups may seem like a lot of vegetable stock for only one cup of peas, but it usually takes this much to get the peas nice and soft. We make this soup all the time, and the amount of vegetable stock needed seems to change with every batch of peas that we get. So, if ten cups isn't enough, add more stock by the cup until the peas are cooked.

| | |
|---|---|
| 4 tbsp olive oil | 2 tomatoes, cored and chopped |
| 2 cooking onions, diced | 1/2 sweet potato, peeled and chopped |
| 4 cloves garlic, minced | 1 cup yellow split peas |
| 4 tbsp minced fresh ginger | 10–16 cups Roasted Vegetable Stock (page 22) |
| 1/2 tsp chili powder | Pinch sea salt |
| 2 tbsp curry powder | Pinch chili powder |

1. Heat oil in a pot over medium heat.
2. Add onions, garlic and ginger. Cook for 5 minutes or until onions are softened.
3. Stir in chili powder and curry powder. Cook for 1 minute.
4. Add tomatoes, sweet potato, split peas and Roasted Vegetable Stock; cook approximately 1 hour or until split peas are soft. Remove from heat. Add salt to taste.
5. Garnish with a shake of chili powder and serve.

SERVES 4–6

# mega miso soup

Making miso soup can be complicated and time consuming if you do it the traditional way, but we have a really easy way that tastes just as good and takes only 5 minutes. Miso soup is perfect for those days when you have a cold and miss the feeling that chicken noodle soup used to give you. Plus, miso soup takes hardly any effort, so even if you're under the weather, it won't seem like too much of a challenge.

Just remember not to boil the miso. Miso is a living food, so boiling it will kill all the enzymes and bacteria that make it good for you.

This is a light soup but can turn into a meal if you add more ingredients. Broccoli, tempeh, spinach, shiitake mushrooms, chickpeas, marinated aramé or hijiki and flakes of nori would all be good additions. If you are using foods that need to be cooked, either cook them in the pot with the water and tamari before adding the miso, or cook them separately and add to the raw ingredients in the bowl.

This recipe makes one large serving; multiply as necessary. If you are having this as an appetizer, or as part of a larger meal, this amount could serve two people.

**BROTH**
2 cups Roasted Vegetable Stock
   (page 22)
2 tsp tamari
3 tbsp miso
1/2 tsp toasted sesame oil

**GARNISHES**
1/4 cup sliced mushrooms
1/2 cup bean sprouts
1/4 cup cilantro, chopped
1 cup cooked soba noodles
1/4 cup carrots, grated
1/8 cup green onions, sliced
8 Marinated Tofu Cubes (page 132)

1.  In a saucepan, bring Roasted Vegetable Stock and tamari to a boil.
2.  Meanwhile, place mushrooms, bean sprouts, cilantro, soba noodles, carrots, green onions and Marinated Tofu Cubes into a large soup bowl.
3.  Remove broth from heat and whisk in miso and toasted sesame oil.
4.  Pour broth over garnishes. Serve.

SERVES 1

# new mexican corn chowder

At the restaurant, we garnish this soup with crispy corn tortillas. If you want to do this at home, slice corn tortillas very thinly, then fry in some hot oil until crisp, which takes only a few seconds. Otherwise, garnish with bought tortillas or corn chips. Or, leave them out altogether, and top the soup with some cilantro and finely chopped red pepper.

| | |
|---|---|
| 2 tbsp olive oil | 1 green pepper, diced |
| 1 cooking onion, diced | 1 lb corn niblets, fresh or frozen |
| 2 cloves garlic, minced | 6 cups Roasted Vegetable Stock (page 22) |
| 1/3 cup white wine | 1 cup cilantro, chopped |
| 1 tsp Cajun seasoning | Pinch sea salt |
| 1 red pepper, diced | |

1. Heat oil in a pot over medium heat.
2. Add onion and garlic. Cook 5 minutes or until browned.
3. Add white wine, and simmer 1 to 2 minutes or until liquid is reduced by half.
4. Stir in Cajun seasoning and red and green peppers; cook 5 minutes or until peppers are slightly softened.
5. Add corn and Roasted Vegetable Stock. Bring to a boil.
6. Remove from heat and add cilantro.
7. Add salt to taste.
8. Remove 1-1/2 cups of the soup and set aside. Using a hand blender, blend rest of soup until smooth. (If you are using a blender, let the soup cool before blending, then reheat.)
9. Add non-puréed soup back to the pot and stir together. Serve.

SERVES 4–6

# mushroom stroganoff soup

This soup is very hearty and rich, and great to serve to people who think they can't be satisfied by a meatless meal.

We garnish this with Tofu Sour Cream, for a traditional touch. The thickening paste gives the soup a velvety texture, but you can leave it out if you wish. We use spelt flour, but you can use whatever flour you have on hand.

2 tbsp olive oil

1 cooking onion, diced

3 cloves garlic, minced

4-1/2 cups button mushrooms, halved

1/3 cup red wine

1-1/2 tsp caraway seeds

4 tsp paprika

1/3 cup tomato paste

4 cups Roasted Vegetable Stock
   (page 22)

1/2 red pepper, diced

1/2 green pepper, diced

1/2 eggplant, diced

1 potato, peeled and diced

Pinch sea salt

6 tbsp Tofu Sour Cream (page 120)

THICKENING PASTE

2 tbsp light spelt flour

1/3 cup filtered water

1. Heat oil in a pot over medium heat.
2. Add onion and garlic; cook 5 minutes over medium heat or until slightly browned.
3. Add mushrooms, and cook 5 minutes or until brown.
4. Add red wine, and simmer 1 to 2 minutes or until liquid is reduced by half.
5. Add caraway seeds, paprika, tomato paste, Roasted Vegetable Stock, red and green peppers, eggplant and potato; bring to a boil.
6. Simmer for approximately 15 minutes, or until all the vegetables are cooked.
7. Mix spelt flour and water in a small bowl. Add a couple of tablespoons of soup to the paste in the bowl and stir until smooth. Continue adding a couple of tablespoons at a time until the paste is the same consistency as the soup. Pour paste into the pot, bring back to a boil and cook for 2 minutes.
8. Add salt to taste.
9. Garnish with Tofu Sour Cream and serve.

SERVES 4–6

# kashmir vegetable soup

This soup gets better with every delicious spoonful. We love its creamy texture, juxtaposed with its pungent exotic spiciness.

Here, we've used a mixture of oil and flour called a "roux" to thicken the soup. But we've gone one step further because we mix flour with flavouring agents to make an "aromatic roux," which adds flavour as well as texture.

| | |
|---|---|
| 4 tbsp olive oil | 1 cup red lentils |
| 2 cooking onions, diced | 1/4 cup tomato paste |
| 6 cloves garlic, minced | 1 cup light spelt flour |
| 1 stalk celery, finely diced | 1 cup canned crushed tomatoes |
| 1 carrot, peeled and finely diced | 8 cups Roasted Vegetable Stock (page 22) |
| 1 tsp cinnamon | 1 cup broccoli, cut into small florets |
| 1 tbsp ground coriander | 1 cup cauliflower, cut into small florets |
| 1 tsp ground red chili flakes | Pinch sea salt |
| 1 tbsp curry powder | |

1. Heat oil in a pot over medium heat.
2. Stir in onions, garlic, celery and carrot. Cook for 1 minute to coat vegetables in oil.
3. Stir in cinnamon, coriander, red chili flakes and curry powder. Cook for 1 minute.
4. Add lentils, tomato paste and flour. Stir for a couple of minutes to cook the flour.
5. Add crushed tomatoes, then Roasted Vegetable Stock gradually, stirring constantly, to avoid lumps.
6. Cook about 15 minutes; when lentils are soft and nearly cooked, add broccoli and cauliflower. Cook another 15 minutes or until vegetables are tender. Add salt to taste.
7. Remove from heat. Serve.

SERVES 4–6

A restaurant that serves good salads will always get repeat customers, in our opinion. Fresh has garnered a reputation for its salads with not only an entire section dedicated to salads and dressings but also many more offered as daily specials. We take our salads very seriously. We aim to help people achieve their goals to eat more fresh vegetables and increase their raw fibre intake. We create varied multi-layered salads and delicious dressings served in huge bowls to satisfy completely. Eating Fresh salads is habit forming, enjoyable and good for your health.

Salads come into their own when treated as a meal rather than as a side dish or afterthought. The secret to a good salad lies in colourful raw ingredients, interesting dressings and tasty toppings. This doesn't necessarily translate into more work, but it requires you to vary your selection of ingredients and choose the right dressing. The world is becoming a smaller place, and now there is an abundance of unique and wonderful produce available. Be unconventional in your choices and you'll be making amazing salads in no time.

We like to use a mix of red leaf, green leaf, Boston, romaine and radicchio for salads at the restaurants. To save time prepping, use a mesclun mix of baby lettuces and baby spinach. These are readily available at most grocery stores. Arugula, endive and fresh herbs are great additions to your salad base. Mix and match according to your taste and mood.

In this section you will find salads topped with main ingredients such as Crispy Tofu, chickpeas, Roasted Potato Wedges, Grilled Tofu Steaks, Marinated Aramé, mango cubes, warm shiitake mushrooms, hummus, and buckwheat and sunflower sprouts. Toasted almonds, pecans, hulled hemp seeds, raw pumpkin seeds, toasted sesame seeds and dried chamomile flowers all provide wonderful and tasty accents to a salad. Finally, choose a delicious dairy-free dressing to clinch your salad experience. These yummy dressings are designed to get you reaching for second and third helpings of fresh salad vegetables.

# salads and dressings

# the raw truth

This salad was inspired by Ruth's first meeting in Hawaii with renowned raw food chef Renée Underkoffler. Because of the tofu, this salad isn't 100 percent raw; however, you can always choose to leave it out. The Wild Ginger Dressing (page 49) is a perfect accompaniment to this salad.

**6 cups mixed lettuce greens**
**1 cup Marinated Tofu Cubes (page 132)**
**1/2 cup buckwheat sprouts**
**1/2 cup sunflower sprouts**
**1/2 cup pea green sprouts**
**1/2 cup Marinated Aramé (page 134)**
**2 tbsp raw pumpkin seeds**

1. Toss lettuce greens, Marinated Tofu Cubes and buckwheat, sunflower and pea green sprouts with the dressing of your choice.
2. Divide and pile into 2 salad bowls.
3. Top each bowl with Marinated Aramé and raw pumpkin seeds. Serve.

SERVES 2

# green destiny

Green Destiny is the name of the magical and all-powerful sword in one of our favourite movies, *Crouching Tiger, Hidden Dragon*. This salad, a recent addition to our menu, is Ruth's favourite salad and was a hit with customers right from the start. This salad always hits the spot, even if you have it every day. The Wild Ginger Dressing (page 49) is a good match.

**4 Marinated Tofu Steaks (page 133)**
**8 cups mixed lettuce greens**
**1/2 cup cucumber, chopped**
**1 cup bean sprouts**
**1/2 cup roasted red peppers, sliced**
**1/2 cup Marinated Aramé (page 134)**
**6 tbsp almonds, sliced and toasted**
**2 tbsp green onions, sliced thinly**

1. Grill or broil the Marinated Tofu Steaks at medium to high heat for 3 minutes or until lightly browned.
2. In a large mixing bowl, toss the lettuce greens, cucumber, bean sprouts, peppers and dressing until well combined. Divide between 2 large salad bowls.
3. In the centre, place Marinated Aramé. Arrange the grilled tofu steaks on either side of the aramé.
4. Garnish with toasted almonds and green onions. Serve.

SERVES 2

# the diva

This Diva sells out every time we have it on special at the restaurant. Some people like it so much that they call ahead to find out if we're serving it!

The Diva was inspired by a salad served at Woodenheads, a fabulous restaurant in Kingston, Ontario. This is the Fresh vegetarian version. We called it the Diva because it's one of our more labour-intensive salads. What really makes this salad special, however, is the combination of warm and crispy potato wedges along with the cool green salad and Creamy Dill Dressing. The capers add just the right amount of tartness to complement the creaminess of the dressing. We recommend using a Yukon Gold or a red-skinned potato—and do leave the peel on.

| | |
|---|---|
| 1 large potato, cut into 8 wedges | 1/2 batch Creamy Dill Dressing (page 51) |
| 2 tbsp olive oil | 6 sun-dried tomatoes, sliced thinly |
| 1/2 tsp sea salt | 2 thin slices red onion |
| 6 cups mixed lettuce greens | 1 ripe avocado, sliced |
| 2 tbsp capers, drained | |

POTATOES

1. Bring a large pot of salted water to a boil.
2. Put potato wedges in and cook until slightly softened, about 7–10 minutes.
3. Drain and shake in the pan to roughen edges (which will help them to crisp later when you roast them). Let cool.
4. When you are ready to make the salad, brush the potato wedges with olive oil, sprinkle with salt and cook at 400ºF. Turn wedges periodically and roast 10 to 15 minutes or until crisp.

SALAD

1. Toss lettuce greens and capers with Creamy Dill Dressing. Divide between 2 salad bowls.
2. Top with sun-dried tomatoes, red onion and avocado.
3. Arrange potato wedges vertically around edges of salad and serve.

SERVES 2

# big salad

This is our version of a house salad—a simple salad with "normal" ingredients. We created the Big Salad for customers who crave a straightforward salad that is delicious and satisfying. Still, we couldn't resist throwing in at least one unusual ingredient, hulled hemp seeds. The name for this salad was inspired by Elaine's favourite lunch on *Seinfeld*. Choose any dressing for this salad.

**8 cups mixed lettuce greens**
**1 red pepper, chopped**
**1/2 cucumber, chopped**
**1 carrot, grated or finely chopped**
**1 avocado, chopped**
**1 tomato, chopped**
**4 tbsp hulled hemp seeds**

1. In a large mixing bowl, toss the lettuce greens, red pepper, cucumber, carrot, avocado, tomato and dressing until well combined.
2. Divide between 2 large salad bowls.
3. Garnish with hulled hemp seeds and serve.

SERVES 2

# peace and love salad

Sounds corny, but it's what we wish for. Lettuce greens, spicy harissa and creamy hummus are a match made in heaven. This salad may be shared as an appetizer on one platter or served in individual portions. For an added dimension, top it with Falafel Ball Mix (page 116) and serve with warm pita bread.

| | |
|---|---|
| **1/4 cup olive oil** | **1 batch Tahini Sauce (page 52)** |
| **4 tbsp tamari** | **1 batch Hummus (page 125)** |
| **6 slices zucchini** | **1 tsp Mixed Herbs (page 124)** |
| **6 slices eggplant** | **1 tsp chili powder** |
| **6 slices sweet potato** | **1 batch Harissa (page 126)** |
| **6 button mushrooms, halved** | **6 slices cucumber** |
| **8 cups mixed lettuce greens** | |

1. Combine olive oil and tamari in a small bowl, and brush zucchini, eggplant, sweet potato and button mushrooms with the mixture.
2. Grill, roast or broil vegetables for 15 to 20 minutes or until tender.
3. Toss lettuce greens with Tahini Sauce. Divide between 2 dinner plates.
4. Place a scoop of Hummus at the centre of each salad. Sprinkle with Mixed Herbs and chili powder.
5. Arrange the grilled vegetables around the Hummus.
6. Put a small dab of Harissa on 3 slices of cucumber and arrange around the edge of each salad. Serve.

SERVES 2

# santa cruz salad

This salad epitomizes light summer eating. Fruits, vegetables, nuts and sprouts all in the same meal will leave you feeling satisfied and energized! To us, Santa Cruz epitomizes the West Coast's laid-back approach to good living and health. Canada's own Santa Cruz is Vancouver, where Ruth's good friend Alison Owen founded Juicy Lucy's, a fantastic juice bar on Commercial Drive.

At the restaurant, we make a "supreme" of oranges by peeling them and then using a sharp paring knife to remove each wedge of flesh from each section. If you don't feel quite up to that, just use canned mandarins!

You can build up this salad nicely with grape tomatoes, chunks of avocado and alfalfa sprouts. Other delicious fruits to be added are blueberries, mango or papaya. We love this with Wild Ginger Dressing (page 49) or Poppy Seed Dressing (page 50).

**8 cups baby spinach**
**2 slices red onion**
**1 cup bean sprouts**
**2 kiwis, peeled and chopped**
**2 oranges, peeled and chopped**
**1/2 cup sliced, toasted almonds**

1. Toss baby spinach, red onion, bean sprouts, kiwis and oranges with dressing. Divide salad between 2 bowls.
2. Garnish with toasted almonds and serve.

SERVES 2

# thai mango salad

If you love mangoes and peanuts as we do, this is the salad for you. If you can't find pea green sprouts, substitute bean sprouts. This salad conjures up images of exotic temples, warm tropical breezes, blue lagoons and white sand beaches.

**6 Marinated Tofu Steaks (page 133)**
**8 cups mixed lettuce greens**
**1/2 batch Spiced Peanut Dressing (page 55)**
**1 fresh mango, peeled, pitted and chopped**
**6 tbsp chopped peanuts**
**6 tbsp chopped cilantro**
**2 cups pea green sprouts**

1.  Grill or broil Marinated Tofu Steaks until lightly browned.
2.  Toss lettuce greens with Spiced Peanut Dressing. Divide between 2 bowls.
3.  Top with mango, chopped peanuts, cilantro, pea green sprouts and grilled tofu steaks. Serve.

SERVES 2

# the bohemian

What is a bohemian? A person living an unconventional life. And this is an unconventional and delightful salad.

We are always on the look out for new, creative toppings for our salads. Dried chamomile flowers have a sweet floral, herbal taste that is a lovely accent to the rest of this salad. Dried calendula flowers are also very pretty and delicious and can be substituted. To use, just crush them slightly with your hand and sprinkle over the salad. Both chamomile and calendula flowers are available at most health food stores, usually in the bulk herb and spice section. The Creamy Sunflower Dressing (page 53) is the perfect complement to this salad.

**16 cubes Marinated Tofu Cubes (page 132)**
**1 batch Crispy Tofu Coating (page 130)**
**3 tbsp olive oil**
**8 cups mixed lettuce greens**
**1/2 cup roasted red pepper, chopped**
**4 tbsp hulled hemp seeds**
**2 tbsp dried chamomile flowers**

1. Toss Marinated Tofu Cubes in Crispy Tofu Coating.
2. Heat olive oil in a skillet over medium heat, add tofu cubes and cook 5 minutes, turning, until browned on all sides.
3. Toss lettuce greens and roasted red pepper with dressing. Divide between 2 bowls.
4. Top with hulled hemp seeds, chamomile flowers and Crispy Tofu Cubes and serve.

SERVES 2

# love nest

We think this salad is very sexy because of the silkiness of cooked shiitakes atop the tangle of aramé and buckwheat sprouts. It's the texture thing that makes this salad sensual. Wild Ginger Dressing (page 49) is perfect for this salad; try serving it piled high on a heavy square Japanese-style plate. Share a bowl of Satori Noodles (page 82) to make this a complete meal.

**4 tbsp olive oil**

**4 cups shiitake mushrooms, stems removed**

**2 tsp tamari**

**6 cups mixed lettuce greens**

**1/2 cup Marinated Aramé (page 134)**

**2 cups buckwheat sprouts**

**2 tbsp sesame seeds, toasted**

1. Heat oil in a skillet over medium heat.
2. Add shiitake mushrooms and tamari. Sauté for 5 minutes or until tender and brown.
3. Toss lettuce greens with dressing. Divide between 2 salad bowls.
4. Top with Marinated Aramé and sautéed mushrooms.
5. Arrange buckwheat sprouts in a pile on the top of each salad. Garnish with toasted sesame seeds and drizzle with a bit more dressing. Serve.

SERVES 2

# flora

This salad is one of our specials and is always very popular, especially at Sunday brunch. It's also one the few salads we serve with one particular dressing. Once you try it, you will see how well these flavours work together.

**4 tbsp olive oil**

**4 cups shiitake mushrooms, stems removed**

**2 tbsp tamari**

**8 cups baby spinach**

**2 cups cooked or canned chickpeas**

**1 cup sunflower sprouts**

**1 cup buckwheat sprouts**

**2 green onions, chopped**

**1/2 batch Poppy Seed Dressing (page 50)**

**6 tbsp toasted pecans**

1. Heat oil in a large skillet.
2. Add shiitake mushrooms and tamari. Sauté for 5 minutes or until tender and brown.
3. Toss baby spinach, chickpeas, sunflower and buckwheat sprouts, and green onions with Poppy Seed Dressing.
4. Divide between 2 salad bowls.
5. Top each salad with sautéed mushrooms and toasted pecans. Serve.

SERVES 2

# wasabi dill dressing

This dressing was developed for the Ninja Rice Bowl (page 61). At that time we were in the midst of our love affair with wasabi, discovering its versatility and adding it to everything. The heat of the wasabi and the coolness of the dill make a great combination, and the sautéed onion and garlic give a depth of flavour that counteracts the blandness of tofu.

We've found that it really makes a difference to mix the water and wasabi first, before adding any other ingredients. This method seems to wake the wasabi up. Otherwise, the wasabi flavour never seems to develop and will just get lost. Store in a sealed container in the fridge for up to three days.

| | |
|---|---|
| 1/4 cup + 1 tbsp olive oil | 2 cups chopped firm tofu |
| 1 cooking onion, thinly sliced | 1 tsp Dijon mustard |
| 3 cloves garlic, minced | 1 tbsp dried dillweed |
| 1 tbsp wasabi powder | 1/4 cup rice vinegar |
| 6 tbsp filtered water | 1/4 tsp sea salt |

1. Heat 1 tablespoon of olive oil in a skillet over medium heat.
2. Sauté onion and garlic for 5 minutes or until softened. Set aside and let cool.
3. Put wasabi and 2 tablespoons water into a blender, and process for 5 seconds to mix.
4. Add onion/garlic mixture, remaining olive oil, chopped firm tofu, Dijon mustard, dillweed, rice vinegar, salt and 2 tablespoons water. Blend until smooth. Add remaining 2 tablespoons water if needed for a pourable consistency.

SERVES 4–6

# wild ginger dressing

The Wild Ginger recipe is inspired by the dressing served over iceberg lettuce at many sushi restaurants, only it's much better. It's really light and fresh, with just a little bite from the ginger. Wild Ginger Dressing goes especially well with the Green Destiny Salad (page 39). You will need a blender to get the proper smooth consistency. Stored in a sealed container in the fridge, it will last at least two weeks.

**1/2 mild onion, chopped**
**1/2 cup sunflower oil**
**1/3 cup rice vinegar**
**2 tbsp filtered water**
**2 tbsp minced fresh ginger**
**1/4 stalk celery**
**1 tbsp tamari**
**1-1/2 tsp raw, unrefined sugar**
**1-1/2 tsp lemon juice**
**1/2 tsp sea salt**
**1/4 tsp ground black pepper**

Combine all ingredients in a blender and process until smooth.

SERVES 4–6

# poppy seed dressing

Not too long ago we tried this dressing on a salad with baby spinach, green leaf lettuce, sunflower seeds, mandarin orange segments, red onion and avocado. It was amazing. There's something about the sweetness of this dressing that, when mixed with savoury things like nuts or seeds and with tart things like mandarins, creates a beautiful harmony of flavour.

Stored in a sealed container in the fridge, it will keep for up to a week.

**3/4 cup raw, unrefined sugar**

**1 tsp dry mustard**

**1 tsp sea salt**

**1/3 cup apple cider vinegar**

**2 tbsp finely chopped onion**

**1 cup sunflower oil**

**4 tsp poppy seeds**

1. Put sugar, mustard, salt, vinegar and onion in a blender, and purée until smooth.
2. With the machine running, add the oil very slowly. Start out with just drops, then gradually increase to a thin stream. This dressing should be quite thick. Pour mixture into bowl.
3. Add poppy seeds and mix well.

SERVES 4–6

# creamy dill dressing

This dressing was developed for The Diva (page 40), but it's delicious on any salad. You may need to add some water to get a nice consistency; this depends on the water content of the tofu you have.

Stored in a sealed container in the fridge, it will last for up to three days.

**1/4 cup + 1 tbsp olive oil**

**1 cooking onion, diced**

**3 cloves garlic**

**2 cups chopped firm tofu**

**1 tbsp dried dillweed**

**1/4 tsp sea salt**

**1 tsp Dijon mustard**

**1/4 cup rice vinegar**

**Filtered water (optional)**

1. Heat 1 tablespoon of oil in a skillet over medium heat.
2. Sauté the onion and garlic for 5 minutes or until softened. Set aside and let cool.
3. Put onion/garlic mixture, remaining olive oil, tofu, dillweed, salt, mustard and vinegar in a blender and process until smooth. Add water if needed for a smooth consistency.

SERVES 4–6

# tahini sauce

This is our most versatile sauce; it tastes great on everything. Tahini is the traditional accompaniment for falafel but can also be used in any kind of stuffed sandwich, or as a salad dressing, or as a sauce with rice bowls or noodles.

Tahini, or sesame butter, is made from ground sesame seeds and is high in protein and a good source of essential fatty acids. You may need to add a bit more water to this recipe if your raw tahini is especially thick. Add water a tablespoon at a time until you get a pourable consistency.

Stored in a sealed container in the fridge, it will last for up to four days.

**2 cloves garlic, minced**
**1/2 cup chopped parsley**
**1/2 tsp sea salt**
**2 tbsp lemon juice**
**2/3 cup filtered water**
**1/2 cup tahini**

1. In a blender, process garlic, parsley, salt and lemon juice until smooth.
2. Add water and tahini. Process until smooth.

SERVES 4–6

# creamy sunflower dressing

If you can't find raw, unsalted sunflower seeds, you can use roasted and salted ones—just leave the salt out of the recipe. Do note that the colour will not come out pure white if roasted seeds are used; it will be more of a tan colour—but it will still taste good.

For a change, try making this dressing with orange or pineapple juice instead of the grapefruit juice.

Stored in a sealed container in the fridge, it will last for up to three days.

**2/3 cup raw sunflower seeds**
**3 cloves garlic, minced**
**1/3 cup grapefruit juice**
**3 tbsp lemon juice**
**1/2 tsp sea salt**
**1 cup filtered water**

Combine all ingredients in a blender and process until smooth and frothy.

SERVES 4–6

# geisha dressing

We are both avid readers and were likely reading *Memoirs of a Geisha* when we named this dressing. Jennifer used to make a dressing similar to this at the Wellington Pub in Kingston, Ontario. The pub doesn't exist anymore but its memory lives on in this dressing. This dressing is best when emulsified (for tips on emulsifying, see page 8).

This dressing is quite strong, so use sparingly. Stored in a sealed container in the fridge, it will last up to two weeks.

**1/4 cup tamari**
**1/4 cup apple cider vinegar**
**1 clove garlic, minced**
**1 tbsp minced fresh ginger**
**1/2 cup olive oil**

1. Pour tamari, vinegar, garlic and ginger in a blender. Process until smooth.
2. While the blender is running, very slowly pour in oil, starting with a drop at a time and gradually increasing to a small stream until all the oil has been incorporated.

SERVES 4–6

# spiced peanut dressing

Sambal oelek is a spicy Indonesian red chili sauce that can be found in specialty shops and Asian groceries. If you can't find it, use whatever kind of hot sauce you have on hand.

Originally created for the Thai Mango Salad (page 44), this is a versatile dressing that works just as well on a cold noodle salad, as a dip for spring rolls, or on any kind of steamed or stir-fried vegetables.

Stored in a sealed container in the fridge, it will last up to four days.

**4 tbsp natural smooth peanut butter**

**4 tbsp filtered water**

**4 tbsp lime juice**

**8 tbsp coconut milk**

**2 tbsp tamari**

**2 tbsp raw, unrefined sugar**

**1/2–1 tsp sambal oelek, depending on how spicy you want it**

Combine all ingredients in a blender and process until smooth.

SERVES 4–6

# caesar dressing

Our vegan version of this classic dressing is rich, creamy and delicious. Serve it with torn romaine lettuce, croutons and kalamata olives, or use it in any kind of tossed salad.

Stored in a sealed container in the fridge, it will last for up to three days.

**1-1/2 tbsp capers**

**2 cloves garlic, minced**

**2 tbsp lemon juice**

**3/4 cup chopped firm tofu**

**2-1/2 tsp Dijon mustard**

**1 tbsp apple cider vinegar**

**1/2 tsp sea salt**

**3/4 tsp ground white pepper**

**1/4 cup filtered water**

**1/2 cup olive oil**

Combine all ingredients in a blender and process until smooth, scraping down the sides occasionally.

SERVES 4–6

# rice bowls

Originating in India, Southeast Asia and China around 4000 B.C., rice is consumed more extensively than any other grain in the world, after wheat. Rich or poor, urban or rural, homes around the globe serve rice. Many cultures have adapted this legendary grain to suit their unique cuisine and cooking styles. At Fresh we have built an entire menu section around the proverbial bowl of rice.

Brown rice contains many nutrients that are all but lost during milling into white rice. Natural unprocessed brown rice contains valuable vitamins and minerals, especially B-vitamins, phosphorous, calcium and potassium. It has a high water content that acts as a natural diuretic to benefit the lymphatic and circulatory systems, and the kidneys.

Unlike polished white rice, natural whole grain (brown) rice comes straight from the fields. Always wash brown rice with cold water until the water runs clear to remove the dust and debris.

Brown rice varieties commonly found in health food stores include short, medium and long grain, sweet and basmati. At Fresh we use steamed brown basmati for our selection of rice bowls. Brown basmati rice is an aromatic long-grain rice native to India and Pakistan and also grown in the southern United States. Basmati is the perfect companion to our many different toppings, sauces and garnishes. For the best presentation and ease of eating, we recommend serving these dishes in a large ceramic rice bowl.

# new buddha rice bowl

This is our most popular rice bowl and one of the first ever created for Fresh by Juice for Life back in the Queen Street Market days. Last year we tinkered with the Buddha Sauce recipe and came up with this new and improved version. The toppings in this dish are also great with soba noodles.

**4 cups cooked brown basmati rice**

**16 Marinated Tofu Cubes (page 132)**

**1-1/2 cups New Buddha Sauce, heated (page 102)**

**2 cups bean sprouts**

**1 tomato, cut into wedges**

**8 slices cucumber, halved**

**1/4 tsp Mixed Herbs (page 124)**

**1/4 tsp Mexican chili powder**

**1/4 cup cilantro, stems removed**

**2 lemon wedges**

1. Divide cooked rice between 2 large rice bowls.
2. Top with Marinated Tofu Cubes.
3. Pour Buddha Sauce over Marinated Tofu Cubes.
4. Arrange bean sprouts, tomato and cucumber on top, then sprinkle with Mixed Herbs and chili powder.
5. Garnish with cilantro and lemon wedges and serve.

SERVES 2

# ninja rice bowl

This is a highly popular and addictive rice bowl. It combines our two most favourite food groups: salad greens and brown rice. We have a sneaking suspicion, however, that it's really the savoury cubes of Crispy Tofu that people are after when they order this dish.

**16 Marinated Tofu Cubes (page 132)**
**1 batch Crispy Tofu Coating (page 130)**
**3 tbsp olive oil**
**2 cups cooked brown basmati rice**
**1-1/2 cups Wasabi Dill Dressing (page 48)**
**8 cups mesclun lettuce mix**
**6 Marinated Sun-Dried Tomatoes, sliced (page 135)**
**1 cup sunflower sprouts**
**2 tbsp Ninja 2 Sauce (page 107)**

1. Toss Marinated Tofu Cubes in Crispy Tofu Coating.
2. Heat olive oil in a skillet over medium heat, add tofu cubes and cook 5 minutes, turning, until browned on all sides.
3. Divide cooked rice between 2 large rice bowls, and drizzle both with half the Wasabi Dill Dressing.
4. Toss mesclun lettuce mix with remaining Wasabi Dill Dressing, and pile on top of rice.
5. Scatter Marinated Sun-Dried Tomato slices on top of lettuce. Make a nest of the sunflower sprouts and put the Crispy Tofu Cubes inside.
6. Drizzle rice bowls with Ninja 2 Sauce and serve.

SERVES 2

# revival rice bowl

The Revival is a comfort food rice bowl combining several high-protein ingredients: peanut sauce, tempeh, hemp seeds and aramé. It is extremely filling and makes a great lunch the next day. For a lighter meal skip the Buddha Sauce and simply drizzle your rice with tamari and olive oil.

**1/3 cup water**

**4 baby bok choy, cut in half lengthwise**

**1 tbsp olive oil**

**1 tbsp tamari**

**4 slices Marinated Tempeh (page 131)**

**4 cups cooked brown basmati rice**

**1-1/2 cups New Buddha Sauce (page 102)**

**1/2 cup Marinated Aramé (page 134)**

**2 green onions, thinly sliced**

**2 tbsp hulled hemp seeds**

1. Put water in a wok or skillet over high heat. Add bok choy halves and cover. Steam 5 minutes until bok choy is almost tender. When water evaporates, add olive oil and tamari; sauté 1 minute until bok choy is tender. Set aside.
2. Grill or broil Marinated Tempeh slices 3 minutes per side or until browned.
3. Divide cooked rice between 2 large rice bowls, and top with Buddha Sauce.
4. Place sautéed bok choy around edges and Marinated Aramé in the middle of each bowl.
5. Arrange grilled tempeh slices on either side of Marinated Aramé. Sprinkle with green onions and hemp seeds. Serve.

SERVES 2

# shanghai rice bowl

The Shanghai is one of our daily special items on rotation at Fresh. This is a tasty rice bowl that always hits the spot. It is easy to prepare.

**1/3 cup water**

**4 baby bok choy, cut in half lengthwise**

**6 tbsp olive oil**

**6 tbsp tamari**

**3 cups shiitake mushrooms, stems removed and halved if large**

**4 cups cooked brown basmati rice**

**1/2 cup Tahini Sauce (page 52)**

**2 tsp Mixed Herbs (page 124)**

**2 cups sunflower sprouts**

**2 tbsp hulled hemp seeds**

**1 cup cooked or canned chickpeas**

**2 lemon wedges**

1. Put water in a wok or skillet over high heat. Add bok choy halves and cover. Steam 5 minutes until bok choy is almost tender. When water evaporates, add 2 tablespoons olive oil, 2 tablespoons tamari and shiitake mushrooms. Sauté 5 minutes until bok choy and mushrooms are tender. Set aside.
2. Divide cooked rice between 2 large rice bowls, and drizzle both with Tahini Sauce, 4 tablespoons olive oil and 4 tablespoons tamari. Sprinkle with Mixed Herbs.
3. Place sautéed bok choy and shiitake mushrooms on rice, and top with sunflower sprouts, hemp seeds and chickpeas.
4. Garnish with lemon wedges and serve.

SERVES 2

# beach rice bowl

This dish was formerly named the Beach Barbeque Rice Bowl because we used to grill the vegetables on skewers. However, we found the skewers took too long to prepare in our busy kitchens and switched to grilling the vegetables directly on the grill. The Beach Rice Bowl has soared in popularity over the last couple of years, mostly because many of our staff love this dish and recommend it every chance they get.

**6 slices eggplant**

**6 slices sweet potato**

**6 slices red pepper**

**6 tbsp olive oil**

**4 cups cooked brown basmati rice**

**3 tbsp tamari**

**2 tsp Mixed Herbs (page 124)**

**6 Marinated Sun-Dried Tomatoes (page 135)**

**6 slices avocado**

**2 cups sunflower sprouts**

**2 wedges lemon**

1. Brush eggplant, sweet potato and red pepper with 1 tablespoon olive oil. Grill or broil for 5 to 10 minutes, until tender, turning vegetables midway. Set aside.
2. Divide cooked rice between 2 large rice bowls, and drizzle both with 2 tablespoons olive oil and 2 tablespoons tamari. Sprinkle with 1 teaspoon Mixed Herbs.
3. Arrange grilled vegetables, Marinated Sun-Dried Tomatoes and avocado on rice.
4. Top with sunflower sprouts.
5. Drizzle with remaining 3 tablespoons olive oil and 1 tablespoon tamari. Sprinkle with remaining 1 teaspoon of Mixed Herbs
6. Garnish with lemon wedges and serve.

SERVES 2

# tantric rice bowl

Don't ask us why we named this rice bowl the Tantric because we probably couldn't put it into words. Suffice to say, we enjoy how we feel after we have eaten this dish.

This is a very simple and straightforward rice bowl to prepare.

**4 cups cooked brown basmati rice**
**1 cup Wasabi Dill Dressing (page 48)**
**1/2 cup Marinated Aramé (page 134)**
**1/2 cup chopped green onions**
**1 cup chopped red peppers**
**1 cup chopped avocado**
**1 cup chopped cucumber**
**2 cups pea green sprouts**
**4 tbsp toasted pumpkin seeds**
**Pinch cayenne pepper**

1. Divide cooked rice between 2 large rice bowls, and drizzle both with half the Wasabi Dill Dressing.
2. Place Marinated Aramé in middle of each rice bowl.
3. Arrange chopped green onions, peppers, avocado and cucumber around edge of each rice bowl. Pile pea green sprouts on top.
4. Sprinkle with toasted pumpkin seeds and cayenne pepper.
5. Drizzle the remaining Wasabi Dill Dressing over each bowl and serve.

SERVES 2

# bliss rice bowl

The Bliss Rice Bowl was one of the first rice bowls on the menu at the original Juice for Life location at the Queen Street Market. Back then it was a simple bowl of brown rice topped with a dollop of guacamole, cilantro and tomato. It has since evolved into a new combination of toppings.

If you are new to pairing avocado with freshly cooked brown rice, prepare yourself; the combination is absolutely divine.

| | |
|---|---|
| 1/3 cup water | 8 slices avocado |
| 4 baby bok choy, cut in half lengthwise | 6 tbsp toasted pumpkin seeds |
| 7 tbsp olive oil | 6 Marinated Sun-Dried Tomatoes, sliced (page 135) |
| 4 tbsp tamari | 1 cup sunflower sprouts |
| 4 cups cooked brown basmati rice | 1 cup buckwheat sprouts |
| 2 tsp Mixed Herbs (page 124) | 2 lemon wedges |
| 2 cups cooked or canned chickpeas | |

1. Put water in a wok or skillet over high heat. Add bok choy halves and cover. Steam 5 minutes until bok choy is almost tender. When water evaporates, add 1 tablespoon olive oil and 1 tablespoon tamari; sauté 1 minute until bok choy is tender. Set aside.
2. Divide cooked rice between 2 large rice bowls, and drizzle both with 3 tablespoons olive oil and 1-1/2 tablespoons tamari. Sprinkle with Mixed Herbs.
3. Top rice with cooked bok choy, chickpeas, avocado, pumpkin seeds, Marinated Sun-Dried Tomatoes, sunflower sprouts and buckwheat sprouts. Drizzle with remaining 3 tablespoons olive oil and 1-1/2 tablespoons tamari.
4. Garnish with lemon wedges and serve.

SERVES 2

# sunflower rice bowl

This rice bowl explores the versatility of sunflower seeds, from raw through toasted to sprouted.

**6 Marinated Tofu Steaks (page 133)**

**1/4 cup filtered water**

**8 cups fresh spinach**

**4 cups cooked brown basmati rice**

**1/2 cup Creamy Sunflower Dressing (page 53)**

**2 cups sunflower sprouts**

**2 tbsp Simple Sauce (page 106)**

**2 tsp Mixed Herbs (page 124)**

**4 tbsp toasted sunflower seeds**

1. Grill or broil Marinated Tofu Steaks for 3 minutes per side or until lightly browned.
2. Put water and spinach in a skillet over high heat. Cover and cook 1 minute, just until spinach is wilted.
3. Divide cooked rice between 2 large rice bowls, and drizzle both with half the Creamy Sunflower Dressing.
4. Top with wilted spinach, grilled tofu steaks and sunflower sprouts.
5. Drizzle with Simple Sauce and remaining Creamy Sunflower Dressing.
6. Sprinkle with Mixed Herbs and toasted sunflower seeds. Serve.

SERVES 2

# hijiki rice bowl

Named after one of our most loved ingredients, this rice bowl is a feast of flavour, texture, colour and nutrients. This is a rice bowl designed to wow your guests.

3 tbsp olive oil

6 Marinated Tofu Steaks (page 133)

1 batch Crispy Tofu Coating (page 130)

4 cups cooked brown basmati rice

1 cup Wasabi Dill Dressing (page 48)

1/2 cup Marinated Hijiki (page 134)

8 slices avocado

1 cup grated carrot

2 cups buckwheat sprouts

2 tbsp toasted sesame seeds

2 lemon wedges

1. Heat olive oil in a wok or skillet over medium heat.
2. Dredge Marinated Tofu Steaks in Crispy Tofu Coating. Cook 2 minutes per side or until browned. Set aside.
3. Divide cooked rice between 2 large rice bowls, and drizzle both with half the Wasabi Dill Dressing.
4. Pile Marinated Hijiki in the middle of the rice. Arrange Crispy Tofu Steaks and avocado slices around it.
5. Place grated carrot around the outer edges of the bowl. Pile buckwheat sprouts on top and sprinkle with sesame seeds.
6. Drizzle with remaining Wasabi Dill Dressing. Garnish with lemon wedges and serve.

SERVES 2

# temple rice bowl

If we acknowledged and treated our bodies with the same care and consideration as we do a place of worship, we would all be a lot healthier. This is a modest rice bowl that will make you feel good. The Hummus, you will discover, goes wonderfully on brown rice.

| | |
|---|---|
| 1/3 cup water | 2 tsp Mixed Herbs (page 124) |
| 4 baby bok choy, cut in half lengthwise | 1 cup Hummus (page 125) |
| 7 tbsp olive oil | 2 cups sunflower sprouts |
| 4 tbsp tamari | 2 tbsp hulled hemp seeds |
| 8 wedges tomato | 4 slices red onion, chopped |
| 4 cups cooked brown basmati rice | 2 lemon wedges |

1. Put water in a wok or skillet over high heat. Add bok choy halves and cover. Steam until bok choy is almost tender. When water evaporates, add 1 tablespoon olive oil, 1 tablespoon tamari and tomato wedges. Sauté 1 minute until bok choy is tender and set aside.

2. Divide cooked rice between 2 large rice bowls. Drizzle both with 6 tablespoons olive oil and 3 tablespoons tamari. Sprinkle with Mixed Herbs.

3. Place Hummus in the middle of each rice bowl, and arrange bok choy around the edge. Top with sunflower sprouts, hemp seeds and red onion.

4. Garnish with lemon wedges and serve.

SERVES 2

# power house

The Power House is for the fast-paced lifestyle of the urban warrior. Packed with nutrition, this excellent meal in a bowl is guaranteed to fuel your body and energize your spirit.

6 Marinated Tofu Steaks (page 133)

1/2 cup Tahini Sauce (page 152)

2 tbsp tamari

1 tsp Hot Sauce (page 105)

4 cups cooked brown basmati rice

1 cup cooked or canned chickpeas

6 slices avocado

1 cup sunflower sprouts

1 cup pea green sprouts

1 cup buckwheat sprouts

2 tbsp toasted sunflower seeds

2 tbsp toasted walnuts

1 tomato, chopped

1/4 cup chopped red onion

1. Grill or broil Marinated Tofu Steaks 3 minutes per side until browned.
2. In a small bowl, mix Tahini Sauce, tamari and Hot Sauce.
3. Divide cooked rice between 2 large rice bowls. Drizzle both with half the sauce.
4. Arrange the Marinated Tofu Steaks, chickpeas, avocado, sprouts, toasted nuts and seeds, tomato and red onion on top of rice.
5. Drizzle with remaining sauce. Serve.

SERVES 2

# gospel rice bowl

Sing hallelujah—come on, get happy! Clap your hands, stamp your feet and give your body something good to eat.

1/3 cup water

4 baby bok choy, cut in half lengthwise

1 tbsp olive oil

1 tbsp tamari

2 cups cooked brown basmati rice

1/2 cup Tahini Sauce (page 52)

2 tbsp toasted nori, torn

2 cups Adzuki Bean Stew (page 114)

10 slices cucumber

2 cups pea green sprouts

2 tbsp toasted sunflower seeds

1. Put water in a wok or skillet over high heat. Add bok choy halves and cover. Steam until bok choy is almost tender. When water evaporates, add olive oil and tamari; sauté 1 minute until bok choy is tender. Set aside.
2. Divide cooked rice between 2 large rice bowls, and drizzle both with half the Tahini Sauce.
3. Sprinkle with torn nori. Top with bok choy, Adzuki Bean Stew, cucumber, pea green sprouts and sunflower seeds.
4. Drizzle with remaining Tahini Sauce and serve.

SERVES 2

# shinto rice bowl

Inspired by a wonderful rice bowl we once had at Wagamama, in London, England. This popular dinner special brings simple ingredients together in a magical way. You will especially enjoy making the Tofu Omelette here. It's an interesting and easy addition to any rice bowl, salad or sandwich.

| | |
|---|---|
| **1/2 cup filtered water** | **2 cups button mushrooms, halved** |
| **2 tbsp + 1 tsp tamari** | **2 cups snow peas, trimmed and cut in half** |
| **2 tsp miso** | **1 cup corn niblets** |
| **2 tbsp olive oil** | **3 cups cooked jasmine rice** |
| **1/4 batch Tofu Omelette (page 152)** | **2 tbsp green onions, thinly sliced** |
| **1 block firm tofu, cut into cubes** | |

1. Heat the water in a pan, add 1 teaspoon tamari and bring to boil. Reduce heat and whisk in miso. Keep warm over low heat.
2. Heat a separate skillet containing 1 tablespoon of the olive oil over medium heat. Press the Tofu Omelette mixture into a thin pancake and sauté 2 minutes per side until browned. Let cool slightly and then cut into thin strips. Set aside.
3. Heat remaining 1 tablespoon olive oil in a wok and add the tofu cubes. Brown tofu on all sides, turning cubes carefully so that they won't break, for approximately 6 to 10 minutes.
4. When tofu is brown, add mushrooms and snow peas, cooking 2 minutes until mushrooms release their liquid and start to brown.
5. Add corn and cook 1 minute until corn is heated through; add rice and 2 tablespoons tamari.
6. Stir to mix vegetables, tofu, rice and tamari and cook until heated through.
7. Divide into two bowls, garnish with green onions and Tofu Omelette strips. Serve with miso broth on the side.

SERVES 2

# noodles

According to the Chinese, long noodles are a symbol of long life. The following Asian-inspired noodle recipes come from the Fresh collection of lunch and dinner specials. We truly love each one of these noodle dishes and would include all of them on the menu every day if only we had the room. Similar to our rice bowls, the secret to our great-tasting noodles lies in the variety of accompaniments: interesting ingredients, mouth-watering sauces and delicious toppings. Each of the following wonderful noodle recipes is a nourishing meal in a bowl.

We use several kinds of noodles as the basis for these dishes. Soba, wheat udon, kamut udon and rice stick noodles are all widely available in Chinese grocery stores and natural food shops.

# samurai soba

These yummy noodles will give you the strength and vigour of a Samurai warrior.

6 Marinated Tofu Steaks (page 133)

4 cloves garlic, minced

1 cup filtered water

4 tbsp tamari

2 cups bok choy, chopped

1 cup Swiss chard, chopped

1 cup kale, chopped

4 cups cooked soba noodles

6 tbsp Creamy Sunflower Dressing (page 53)

1 cup sunflower sprouts

1 tbsp sunflower seeds, toasted

1 tbsp toasted sesame seeds

1. Grill or broil Marinated Tofu Steaks 3 minutes per side until browned. Set aside.
2. Place garlic, water, tamari, bok choy, Swiss chard and kale in a wok or skillet over high heat. Cook 2 minutes until greens are tender.
3. Add soba noodles and cook 2 minutes until heated through and most of the cooking liquid has evaporated.
4. Divide cooked noodles and vegetables between 2 large bowls and top with grilled tofu steaks.
5. Drizzle with Creamy Sunflower Dressing.
6. Garnish with sunflower sprouts, sunflower seeds and sesame seeds. Serve.

SERVES 2

# wildfire

This dish is named Wildfire because it's best really spicy! The Creamy Sunflower Dressing adds a cooling note. The amount of sambal oelek called for in this recipe will make it, in our estimation, medium spicy, but use your own judgment. Rice stick noodles are flat and opaque, made from rice flour and water.

**6 slices Marinated Tempeh (page 131)**

**4 tbsp olive oil**

**4 cloves garlic, minced**

**1 tomato, chopped**

**3 tsp sambal oelek**

**4 tbsp Bragg's Liquid Aminos or tamari**

**4 cups rice stick noodles (page 8),
  soaked and drained**

**1 cup filtered water**

**2 cups bok choy, chopped**

**1 cup Swiss chard, chopped**

**1 cup kale, chopped**

**2 tbsp hulled hemp seeds**

**6 tbsp Creamy Sunflower Dressing (page 53)**

1. Grill or broil Marinated Tempeh for 3 minutes per side until browned.
2. Heat olive oil in a skillet over medium heat. Add garlic and chopped tomato. Cook for 1 minute.
3. Add sambal oelek, Bragg's Liquid Aminos, noodles, water, bok choy, Swiss chard and kale.
4. Bring to a boil and cook 3 minutes until noodles are tender. Stir frequently.
5. Divide noodle mixture between 2 large bowls. Top with tempeh, hemp seeds and Creamy Sunflower Dressing. Serve.

SERVES 2

# tsunami

"Tsunami" is the Japanese word for tidal wave. The hijiki, a sea-harvested vegetable, reminds us of the ocean; hence, the name.

Kamut udon noodles are a good choice for anyone with a wheat allergy. Created as an alternative to the traditional wheat udon, kamut udon are most often found in health food stores.

| | |
|---|---|
| **4 cups cooked kamut udon noodles** | **1 cup grated carrot** |
| **1/2 cup Tahini Sauce (page 52)** | **2 cups sunflower sprouts** |
| **2 tsp Hot Sauce (page 105)** | **4 tbsp cilantro, chopped** |
| **1/2 cup Marinated Hijiki (page 134)** | **2 tbsp toasted sesame seeds** |
| **1 avocado, sliced** | **2 lemon wedges** |

1. Divide cooked udon noodles between 2 large bowls, and drizzle with half the Tahini Sauce and 1 teaspoon Hot Sauce.
2. Pile Marinated Hijiki in the middle of bowl, and arrange avocado, grated carrot, sunflower sprouts and cilantro around the edges.
3. Sprinkle with sesame seeds and drizzle with remaining Tahini and Hot Sauce.
4. Garnish with lemon wedges. Serve.

SERVES 2

# big green

This is one of our most popular nightly noodle specials. If you can't find the kamut udon, use any kind of long noodle or pasta.

1/3 cup filtered water

4 baby bok choy, cut into halves lengthwise

2 cloves garlic, minced

1 tbsp olive oil

1 tsp tamari

6 Marinated Tofu Steaks (page 133)

4 cups cooked kamut udon noodles

2 green onions, finely sliced

1/4 red pepper, finely diced

2 tbsp toasted sesame seeds

6 tbsp Sesame Miso Sauce (page 109)

1. Put water and bok choy in a wok or skillet over medium heat. Steam for 5 minutes until bok choy is almost tender. When water evaporates, reduce heat and add garlic, olive oil and tamari.

2. Sauté 1 minute until bok choy is tender.

3. Grill or broil Marinated Tofu Steaks 3 minutes per side until browned.

4. Divide noodles between 2 large bowls.

5. Top with bok choy, grilled tofu steaks, green onions, red pepper and sesame seeds.

6. Drizzle with Sesame Miso Sauce. Serve.

SERVES 2

# emerald city

This dish uses gochujang, a Korean fermented chili paste with a unique flavour and bright red colour. It is available at some supermarkets and at most Asian groceries. If you can't find it, substitute a bit of hot sauce—it won't give you the same flavour as gochujang, but it'll still be delicious.

Emerald City was named by Ryan Kelly, a multi-talented former staff member, after the city in *The Wizard of Oz*.

| | |
|---|---|
| 2 tbsp olive oil | 1/2 cup filtered water |
| 2 cups button mushrooms, sliced | 4 cups cooked kamut udon noodles |
| 2 tsp balsamic vinegar | 4 cups fresh spinach |
| 4 cloves garlic, minced | 6 tbsp Pineapple Cashew Sauce (page 108) |
| 1 tsp gochujang (Korean chili paste) | 4 tbsp toasted cashews |
| 4 tbsp tamari | 1 cup sunflower sprouts |

1. In a pan, heat olive oil over low heat and add mushrooms and balsamic vinegar. Cook 5 minutes until browned and mushrooms are tender.
2. In a separate wok or skillet, mix garlic, gochujang, tamari, water, noodles and spinach. Cook 2 minutes until heated through, liquid is reduced and spinach is tender.
3. Divide noodle mixture between 2 large bowls and top with mushrooms.
4. Drizzle with Cashew Pineapple Sauce.
5. Garnish with toasted cashews and sunflower sprouts. Serve.

SERVES 2

# ponzu noodles

This combination of vegetables, cashews and noodles is a simple, light and delicious meal. Jennifer once took some of this home from work one day, and her roommate's friend ate it. Even years later, whenever she sees him, he asks when she'll bring him more of these noodles!

2 tbsp olive oil

1-1/2 cups shiitake mushrooms, stems removed and halved if large

1-1/2 cups button mushrooms, halved

6 cups broccoli florets

1/2 cup filtered water

1/2 batch Ponzu Sauce (page 103)

4 cups cooked soba noodles

1/2 cup roasted cashews

1/4 cup red pepper, finely diced

2 tbsp toasted sesame seeds

1. Heat oil in a skillet over high heat. Add all mushrooms and cook 3 minutes until browned.
2. Add broccoli and water. Cook 5 minutes until water evaporates.
3. Add Ponzu Sauce and bring to a boil. When broccoli is almost tender, add noodles and cashews. Stir.
4. Cook 2 minutes until heated through.
5. Divide between 2 large bowls. Garnish with diced red pepper and sesame seeds. Serve.

SERVES 2

# satori noodles

The word "satori" means "the moment of enlightenment" in Zen Buddhism. We hope your body will feel enlightened after eating these sweet spicy noodles.

**1/3 cup filtered water**

**4 baby bok choy, cut in half lengthwise**

**1 tbsp tamari**

**3 tbsp olive oil**

**4 cups shiitake mushrooms, stems removed and halved if large**

**4 strips Marinated Tempeh, chopped (page 131)**

**4 cups rice stick, soaked and drained (page 8)**

**2 cups Satori Sauce (page 104)**

**4 tbsp cilantro, chopped**

**2 tbsp toasted sesame seeds**

1. Place water and bok choy in a skillet. Steam 5 minutes until water is evaporated and bok choy is almost tender. Add the tamari and 1 tablespoon olive oil; cook 1 minute until tender. Set aside.
2. In a separate pan, heat 2 tablespoons olive oil. Add shiitake mushrooms and Marinated Tempeh. Cook 3 minutes until mushrooms are tender.
3. Add rice stick and Satori Sauce. Cook 3 minutes until noodles are tender, stirring occasionally.
4. Divide noodle mixture between 2 bowls and top with bok choy.
5. Garnish with cilantro and sesame seeds. Serve.

SERVES 2

# supreme udon noodles

Here is another great use for Satori Sauce. Some of the ingredients for this dish are not widely available, but if you live in a city with a good Korean market, you are in luck. Fresh udon, fat round wheat noodles, are found in the frozen food section, usually in packages of five individual portions. They cook quickly in about a minute: just bring water to a boil, dunk noodles in, and as soon as they are thawed, drain them.

Vegetable dumplings, also known as potstickers, are usually found in the same frozen section. Check the ingredients carefully to choose a brand without MSG. Potstickers are quite fragile and have a tendency to rip open if you are too rough when handling them. Tempeh or tofu makes a good substitute.

Any leftover dumplings make a good appetizer for another meal. Just sauté or steam them, and serve with Spiced Peanut Dressing (page 55) for dipping.

| | |
|---|---|
| 12 vegetable dumplings | 1/2 cup filtered water |
| 2 tbsp olive oil | 2 portions fresh udon noodles, cooked |
| 2 cups button mushrooms, sliced | 1-1/2 cups Satori Sauce (page 104) |
| 2 cups bok choy, chopped | 2 tbsp toasted sesame seeds |
| 1 cup kale, chopped | 2 tbsp toasted nori, torn into small pieces |
| 1 cup Swiss chard, chopped | |

1. In a steamer, steam the vegetable dumplings for 5 minutes. Set aside.
2. Heat the olive oil in a skillet over medium to high heat and add mushrooms. Cook 3 minutes until browned.
3. Add bok choy, kale, Swiss chard and water; sauté 2 minutes until greens are tender and water evaporates. Add cooked noodles and Satori Sauce. Cook 2 minutes until heated through.
4. Divide between 2 large bowls. Top with steamed dumplings, sesame seeds and toasted nori. Serve.

SERVES 2

# jeya's special noodles

Prapa, one of our longtime cooks, showed Jen how to make these noodles. Jeya, our head dishwasher, and the backbone of our Bloor Street operation, likes to have them almost every day for his lunch. Jennifer took it as a great compliment the day that one of our brigade of Sri Lankan kitchen staff exclaimed, "Jennifer understands Sri Lankan noodles!"

These noodles are great as is, but we also like them with Creamy Sunflower Dressing (page 53) drizzled on top.

| | |
|---|---|
| **4 tbsp olive oil** | **4 tbsp tamari** |
| **1 cup zucchini, diced** | **2 tbsp curry powder** |
| **1/2 cup red pepper, diced** | **2 tsp Hot Sauce (page 105)** |
| **1/2 cup green pepper, diced** | **1 cup filtered water** |
| **1 cup broccoli, chopped** | **4 cups rice stick, soaked and drained (page 8)** |
| **1/2 cup tomato, chopped** | **2 cups bean sprouts** |
| **1 cup mushrooms, sliced** | **2 tbsp cilantro, chopped** |
| **4 cloves garlic, minced** | **2 lemon wedges** |
| **1/2 cup red onion, chopped** | |

1. Heat oil in a wok or skillet over medium-low heat. Add zucchini, red pepper, green pepper, broccoli, tomato, mushrooms, garlic, red onion and tamari; sauté until softened.
2. Add curry powder and Hot Sauce. Stir for half a minute.
3. Add water and rice stick. Cook over high heat for 3 minutes until noodles are tender and most of the liquid has evaporated, stirring often.
4. Divide noodle mixture between 2 bowls. Garnish with bean sprouts, cilantro and lemon wedges.

SERVES 2

# sandwiches

A simple sandwich can be incredibly pleasing and filling. However, a sandwich's success depends on three important components: fresh bread, a good spread and the right filling.

Developing delectable and varied vegetarian sandwiches can be a challenge if you don't want to simply use the same ingredients over and over. The Fresh sandwich menu has developed slowly; each sandwich has had to prove itself first as a daily special before it graduated to the main menu. This process has yielded excellent results: we now have a stable of unusual ingredients, tasty spreads and a variety of breads to choose from.

The following 12 sandwiches are guaranteed to satisfy; however, they are even more substantial accompanied by soup or salad.

# reality bites

The Reality Bites is a toasted triple-decker layered sandwich. It's a great lunch-time sandwich that packs well, if you use toothpicks to secure it.

**12 slices multi-grain bread**
**1/2 batch Herb Tofu Mayo (page 128)**
**4 leaves lettuce**
**2 avocados, sliced**
**12 slices tomato**
**4 slices red onion**
**2 cups alfalfa sprouts**

1. Toast bread and spread each slice with Herb Tofu Mayo.
2. On 4 slices, place lettuce, avocado and tomato. Top with second slice of bread.
3. On the second slices, place red onion and alfalfa sprouts. Top with remaining bread and cut in half diagonally. Secure with toothpicks and serve.

SERVES 4

# bbq tempeh wrap

This sandwich is a bit messy, but it's so yummy that it's worth it. This is a good thing to serve someone who is reluctant to try tempeh, or who thinks that a meal without meat can't be satisfying.

Serving this as a wrap makes it a bit tidier, but you can serve it on crusty sourdough bread—just be sure to have plenty of napkins on hand! If you can't find 12-inch tortillas, use smaller ones and serve two per person.

**1/4 cup canola oil**

**2 green peppers, sliced**

**2 cooking onions, sliced**

**8 slices Marinated Tempeh (page 131), chopped diagonally into bite-size pieces**

**1 batch BBQ Sauce (page 112)**

**4 12-inch whole wheat tortillas**

**1 batch Honey Mustard Mayo (page 123)**

**4 cups shredded lettuce**

**2 tomatoes, sliced**

1. Heat oil in a skillet on medium heat.
2. Add green pepper and onion. Cook for 5 minutes or until softened.
3. Add Marinated Tempeh and cook for 1 minute.
4. Stir in BBQ Sauce, and cook until heated through. Set aside.
5. Warm tortillas on a grill or in the oven.
6. Spread tortillas with Honey Mustard Mayo, and then top with shredded lettuce and tomato.
7. Add tempeh mixture.
8. Roll tortillas, folding in both ends. Cut in half and serve.

SERVES 4

# magic tofu sandwich

The current favourite at Fresh is our Crispy Tofu. In the Ninja Rice Bowl (page 61) crispy tofu cubes appear as a topping, and here we have crispy tofu steaks sandwiched in a whole-grain bun with other tasty sandwich fixings.

Alfalfa sprouts will do nicely if you can't find buckwheat sprouts.

1/4 cup canola oil

8 Marinated Tofu Steaks (page 133)

1 batch Crispy Tofu Coating (page 130)

4 whole-grain buns, sliced in half

1 batch Honey Mustard Mayo (page 123)

2 cups buckwheat sprouts

2 medium tomatoes, sliced

4 slices red onion

1/2 cup grated carrot

1. Heat oil in pan over medium heat.
2. Dredge Marinated Tofu Steaks in Crispy Tofu Coating until totally coated.
3. Cook tofu steaks in the pan for 2 minutes per side or until browned. Set aside.
4. Toast buns. Spread both halves of each with Honey Mustard Mayo.
5. Top with buckwheat sprouts, tomato, red onion, carrot and crispy tofu steaks.
6. Cut sandwiches in half and serve.

SERVES 4

# the big zim

This triple-decker sandwich was named for Mark Zimmerman, a good friend and regular customer, because he was always wishing that we had more eggplant on the menu. Jennifer, for the record, has a strong bias against using eggplant; she believes they have become cliché and are probably the most overused vegetable in the world of traditional vegetarian cooking. The Big Zim, however, saves the day with a new delicious approach.

When you taste this, you may notice an uncanny similarity to a famous fast-food sandwich. Although this wasn't our goal, this sandwich does prove that you don't have to use animal products to get the same familiar fast-food flavours that we all crave sometimes.

At the restaurants we prep the eggplant ahead of time, salting both sides and dabbing off the moisture that is released. We find this makes a big difference in the tenderness of the eggplant. If you don't have time for this step, just cook the eggplant a little longer to ensure it is soft.

| | |
|---|---|
| 1 eggplant, cut in 1/4-inch slices | 4 lettuce leaves |
| 1 batch Crispy Tofu Coating (page 130) | 1 tomato, sliced |
| 6 tbsp canola oil | 8 slices kosher dill pickle |
| 12 slices multi-grain bread | 1/4 red onion, sliced |
| 1 batch Special Sauce (page 113) | 8 toothpicks |

1. Dredge slices of eggplant in Crispy Tofu Coating and set aside.
2. Heat oil in a pan over medium heat. Add eggplant and sauté both sides until brown.
3. Toast multi-grain bread.
4. Spread Special Sauce on slices of toasted bread.
5. On 4 slices of toast, place lettuce and eggplant slices. Add a second slice of toast to each sandwich, and place tomato, pickles and onions on top. Top with the last slice of toast.
6. Cut sandwich in half diagonally, and hold in place with toothpicks. Serve.

SERVES 4

# soho sandwich

Portobello mushrooms are like steak for vegetarians. You may think they're expensive, but when you compare them to real steak, they're an absolute bargain.

Portobello mushrooms are similar to tofu in their versatility. For something different, brush the mushrooms with a bit of BBQ Sauce (page 112) instead of the balsamic vinegar and olive oil. Or, for a spicier version, you can brush the mushrooms with a bit of chipotle pepper that you may have left over from the Southwestern Polenta (page 145).

If you can't get sunflower sprouts, substitute alfalfa, radish or broccoli sprouts.

**4 large portobello mushroom caps, washed**

**4 tbsp balsamic vinegar**

**4 tbsp olive oil**

**Pinch sea salt**

**4 whole-grain buns, sliced in half**

**1 batch Honey Mustard Mayo (page 123)**

**2 cups sunflower sprouts**

**1 tomato, sliced**

**1/4 red onion, sliced**

1. Drizzle both sides of mushroom caps with balsamic vinegar, olive oil and a pinch of salt.
2. Cook mushroom caps on a grill, in a skillet or under a broiler for 5 minutes per side, until tender.
3. Toast buns and spread with Honey Mustard Mayo.
4. Place the sprouts, tomato and onion on bottom of buns. Place mushrooms on top.
5. Top with upper half of bun and cut in half. Serve.

SERVES 4

# wrapper's delight

This sandwich is named after Jennifer's favourite song from the 1970s, and the only song she has ever performed in a karaoke bar!

This is a perfect wrap for a light summer lunch. It is so simple to make but is a change from the usual sandwich format. Substitute tomato or spinach tortillas if you prefer. If you can't find 12-inch tortillas, use smaller ones and serve two per person.

**4 12-inch whole wheat tortillas**
**1 batch Honey Mustard Mayo (page 123)**
**1 batch Marinated Tofu Cubes (page 132)**
**1 avocado, sliced**
**2 tomatoes, chopped**
**1/4 red onion, sliced**
**1/2 cucumber, chopped**
**8 cups lettuce, shredded**

1. Heat tortillas on a grill or in the oven for 1 minute or until just warmed through.
2. Spread each tortilla with Honey Mustard Mayo.
3. Top with Marinated Tofu Cubes, avocado, tomatoes, red onion, cucumber and lettuce.
4. Roll tortillas, folding in the ends, and cut in half. Serve.

SERVES 4

# voodoo sandwich

When Jennifer was a little girl, she had an argument with her friend Kathi Glatt about the term "kaiser bun." Because Jennifer's mum is British, Jennifer had only ever heard the word pronounced "kaisa," so when she told her friend what they were having for lunch, naturally she pronounced it "kaisa." They proceeded to argue about it the whole way home, until they asked Jen's mum to spell it. Needless to say, Jen had to admit she was wrong, something she doesn't like to do to this day!

This sandwich is yummy whether you have it on a kaiser, ciabatta or panini bun.

**1/4 cup olive oil**

**4 cups mushrooms, sliced**

**1 red onion, sliced thinly**

**2 tbsp tamari**

**4 tbsp Hot Sauce (page 105)**

**1 9 oz (250 g) block firm tofu, cut into 4 slices**

**4 whole-grain buns, sliced in half**

**1/2 batch Honey Mustard Mayo (page 123)**

**4 cups alfalfa sprouts**

1. Heat oil in a large pan or skillet.
2. Add mushrooms and onion. Cook 3 minutes until browned.
3. Add tamari, Hot Sauce and tofu slices. Stir. Cook until tofu is browned and hot, being careful not to break the slices.
4. Toast buns and spread both halves of each with Honey Mustard Mayo.
5. Place alfalfa sprouts on bottom half of buns.
6. Top with tofu mixture and other half of buns. Serve.

SERVES 4

# bermuda triangle

Rich Brown, Ruth's hubby, came up with the name for this sandwich. As a drummer, Rich had toured in Bermuda, and this sandwich, with its sweet potato and hot sauce, reminded him of island cuisine. Incidentally, the father of a close friend of theirs actually disappeared flying over the Bermuda Triangle many years before.

If you can't find focaccia, use whatever bread you like. This sandwich would also be delicious with lettuce, sliced tomato and avocado.

**8 slices sweet potato**
**1/4 cup + 1 tbsp olive oil**
**4 cups sliced mushrooms**
**1 red onion, sliced thinly**
**2 tbsp tamari**
**4 tbsp Hot Sauce (page 105)**
**1 round focaccia, cut into 4 wedges**
**1/2 batch Honey Mustard Mayo (page 123)**
**4 cups alfalfa sprouts**

1. Brush sweet potato on both sides with 1 tablespoon of olive oil. Grill or bake 5 to 10 minutes until tender. (Alternatively, steam the slices for 5 minutes or until tender, in which case you will not need the oil.) Set aside.
2. Heat remaining oil in a large pan.
3. Add mushrooms and onion, and sauté 3 minutes until browned.
4. Add tamari and Hot Sauce. Cook 1 minute or until most of the liquid has evaporated.
5. Cut the focaccia wedges in half horizontally. Spread each wedge with Honey Mustard Mayo.
6. Place alfalfa sprouts on 4 halves of focaccia. Top with grilled sweet potato, mushrooms and onions.
7. Top with remaining focaccia and cut in half. Serve.

SERVES 4

# coconut curry wrap

This hot and spicy wrap is a great way to use up leftover rice. If you can't find 12-inch tortillas, use smaller ones and serve two per person.

**3 tsp olive oil**
**12 slices sweet potato**
**4 12-inch whole-wheat tortillas**
**4 cups cooked brown basmati rice**
**8 cups mixed lettuce**
**1/2 batch Coconut Curry Sauce (page 110)**
**3/4 cup Tahini Sauce (page 52)**

1. Brush sweet potato slices with oil and grill or bake for 5 to 10 minutes until tender. (Alternatively, steam the slices for 5 minutes or until tender, in which case you will not need the oil.) Chop into bite-sized pieces. Set aside.
2. Heat tortillas on a grill or in the oven for 1 minute or until just warmed through.
3. Top each tortilla with cooked rice, lettuce, chopped sweet potato, Coconut Curry Sauce and Tahini Sauce.
4. Roll tortillas, folding the ends in. Cut in half and serve.

SERVES 4

# adzuki wrap

This hot wrap is very filling and highly nutritious. Combining adzuki beans and whole wheat tortilla makes this a good protein option. If you can't find 12-inch tortillas, use smaller ones and serve two per person.

**4 12-inch whole wheat tortillas**
**8 cups mixed lettuce**
**2 cups alfalfa sprouts**
**4 cups carrot, grated**
**1 avocado, sliced**
**4 cups Adzuki Bean Stew (page 114)**
**1/2 batch Creamy Sunflower Dressing (page 53)**

1. Heat tortillas on a grill or in the oven for 1 minute or until just warmed through.
2. Arrange lettuce, sprouts, carrot and avocado in the middle of each tortilla.
3. Top with Adzuki Bean Stew and a drizzle of the Creamy Sunflower Dressing.
4. Roll tortillas, folding the ends in. Cut in half and serve.

SERVES 4

# power lunch

If you ever feel a hankering for a tuna salad sandwich, try this instead. It's high in protein, carbs and flavour.

**8 slices multi-grain bread**
**1 batch Chickpea Spread (page 129)**
**4 tbsp sunflower seeds, toasted**
**1 roasted red pepper, cut in strips**
**4 cups mixed lettuce**
**2 cups alfalfa sprouts**

1. Toast bread.
2. Divide the chickpea salad between 4 slices of toasted bread.
3. Sprinkle with sunflower seeds and then top with roasted red pepper, lettuce, alfalfa sprouts and remaining slices of toasted bread. Serve.

SERVES 4

# falafel in a pita

Ruth lived on a kibbutz in Israel, farming cotton, for five years when she was in her early 20s. Needless to say, she fell in love with falafel and all foods of Middle Eastern origin.

Falafel is the most popular fast food in Israel, and falafel stands can be found lining the highways, clustered around bus stations, and in city, town and village markets. Each stand is owner-operated, and great pride is taken in the taste and quality of one's falafel and pita and in the variety of accompaniments. Customers can stuff their pitas with as many accompaniments and toppings as can fit. Options include tahini sauce, fresh veggies, fried eggplant, hot peppers, olives and pickled lemons. Falafel is a high-protein, inexpensive, quick bite that also travels well.

**4 whole-grain Middle Eastern pita, warmed**

**2 cups alfalfa sprouts**

**2 medium tomatoes, chopped**

**1 cup chopped cucumber**

**4 slices red onion**

**1/2 cup chopped parsley**

**16 Falafel Balls (page 116)**

**1 cup Tahini Sauce (page 52)**

**Pinch cayenne pepper**

1. Slice off top 2 inches of pita and open up to form a pocket.
2. Stuff pita with alfalfa, tomato, cucumber, red onion, parsley and Falafel Balls.
3. Drizzle with Tahini Sauce and sprinkle with cayenne pepper.

SERVES 4

# sauces and mixes

Sauces make the dish. No one wants to eat a bowl of plain rice—not even the contestants on *Survivor*. It's the sauce that makes the meal enjoyable. Take the most mundane ingredients, add a great sauce, and presto, you have a tasty meal.

Our sauces range from light to creamy, and spicy to sweet. However, all are delicious and simple to make. And even though we do use some classic French culinary techniques, don't be intimidated—our recipes are designed to be simple. We don't have time to fool around with complicated recipes, and we're sure you don't either.

Our stews and mixes are all bean-based and provide a protein-rich element in many of our recipes.

# new buddha sauce

This is our new and improved Buddha Sauce. It is the basis for our popular New Buddha Rice Bowl (page 60) and Revival Rice Bowl (page 62). But it has myriad other uses too. Use it cold or hot as a dip for fries, spring rolls and grilled vegetable skewers. Heated, it makes a great topping for noodles and rice.

This sauce lasts about five days in the fridge and also freezes well. Be careful when heating it; stir often as the peanut butter has a tendency to burn. To reheat, you may need to whisk in some water to get the right consistency and to prevent scorching. If you don't have a juicer, replace the carrot juice with Roasted Vegetable Stock (page 22).

| | |
|---|---|
| 3 tbsp olive oil | 3/4 cup rice vinegar |
| 1 cooking onion, diced | 1 cup filtered water |
| 6 tbsp minced fresh ginger | 2 cups natural smooth peanut butter |
| 6 cloves garlic | 1/4 cup lemon juice |
| 2 tsp curry powder | 2/3 cup tamari |
| 1 tsp cayenne pepper | 2 tbsp toasted sesame oil |
| 1-1/3 cups carrot juice | 1/4 cup sunflower oil |

1. Heat oil in a pot. Add onion, ginger and garlic. Cook 5 minutes or until onion is soft.
2. Add curry powder and cayenne pepper. Cook for 2 minutes. Remove from heat.
3. Add remaining ingredients. Stir and let cool. Purée in a blender until smooth.
4. Before serving, heat gently in a saucepan over low heat.

SERVES 6

# ponzu sauce

This is the secret sauce behind our Ponzu Noodles (page 81). It is also the base for the Satori Sauce (page 104). It has a mouth-watering subtle flavour and will keep in the fridge for about a month!

This sauce requires straining out the solids and keeping the liquid, the opposite of what we normally do in a restaurant. Whenever we make this, we're always afraid that we're going to drain the liquid right down the sink and keep the solids. Believe us, it's happened to more than one cook over the years!

**8 cloves garlic, smashed**

**1/2 cup coarsely chopped fresh ginger**

**3 stalks lemon grass, roughly chopped into 1/2-inch pieces**

**1/2 tsp crushed chili flakes**

**1/2 cup white wine**

**4 cups filtered water**

**3/4 cup tamari**

**3/4 cup raw, unrefined sugar**

1. Combine all ingredients in a pot and bring to a boil, stirring until sugar dissolves.
2. Reduce heat and simmer for 20 minutes.
3. Strain, reserving liquid and discarding solids.

SERVES 4

# satori sauce

Lemon grass is easy to use; just cut off the root end and the thin straggly bits at the other end. Peel off the outer layer and keep peeling until you get to a nice fresh-looking layer. Lay it on the counter and, with the blunt side of your knife, whack the length of stalk until it starts to break apart and release its aroma. Chop into 1-inch pieces and use for cooking. Lemon grass is not usually eaten, because it is so tough. However, by straining it out, you still have its aroma and taste.

Cornstarch, in small quantities, is a good thickener but must be cooked thoroughly to rid it of that raw taste. Cornstarch must always be dissolved in water or another liquid before adding it to any sauce. Always bring a sauce back to a boil and simmer for a couple of minutes after adding cornstarch.

**1 batch Ponzu Sauce (page 103)**
**1 cup Roasted Vegetable Stock (page 22)**
**1 tsp sambal oelek**
**1 clove garlic, minced**
**5 tbsp cornstarch**

1. Place Ponzu Sauce in a saucepan, and add 1/2 cup Roasted Vegetable Stock, sambal oelek and garlic. Bring to a boil.
2. Dissolve cornstarch in remaining 1/2 cup of stock and stir. Add to the pot.
3. Bring sauce back to a boil, and simmer for 2 minutes until thickened to cook the cornstarch.
4. Remove from heat.

SERVES 6

# hot sauce

This hot sauce has tons of flavour, not just heat. It was invented by Stash, a long-time friend of Ruth's. He was nice enough to share the recipe with us, and we have incorporated it into many of our daily specials.

Scotch bonnets are really hot! You've probably heard the horror stories about people who worked with hot chilies and then rubbed their eyes, or even worse, went to the bathroom! This is all true; the burn can last for hours. Luckily, in this recipe, you won't even need to touch the peppers, except to remove stems if there are any.

If you can't find Scotch bonnets, use whatever fresh chilies you can find, but the sauce won't be quite as hot.

Capsaicin, one of the chemical components of hot chilies, is addictive and gives a kind of high. That's why people who are addicted to hot spices insist on always eating their food this way.

This sauce keeps indefinitely in the fridge.

| | |
|---|---|
| 4 Scotch bonnet peppers | 1/4 cup balsamic vinegar |
| 1/2 red onion, chopped | 1 stalk lemon grass, trimmed and |
| 2 green onions, chopped | chopped into 3-inch pieces |
| 2 cloves garlic | 1/4 cup Dijon mustard |
| 1/2 inch fresh ginger | 1/2 tsp curry powder |
| 1 sprig thyme, leaves removed | 1/2 tsp cayenne pepper |
| from woody stems | 1/2 tsp crushed chilies |
| 1 sprig rosemary, leaves removed | 1/4 tsp oregano |
| from woody stems | 1/4 tsp cinnamon |
| 1/2 cup tamari | 1/4 tsp ground cumin |

1. Purée Scotch bonnets, red onion, green onions, garlic, ginger, thyme and rosemary in a food processor.
2. Pour the purée into a saucepan and add tamari. Cook over low heat for about 5 minutes, or until mixture turns dark brown.
3. Add balsamic vinegar, lemon grass, Dijon mustard, curry powder, cayenne pepper, chilies, oregano, cinnamon and cumin. Bring to a boil and simmer 30 minutes.
4. Remove from heat and cool. Serve.

SERVES 8

# simple sauce

This intensely flavoured sauce is the base for the Ninja 2 Sauce (page 107) and is also used to marinate the Aramé and Hijiki (page 134). It is great splashed on steamed greens, brown rice and noodle dishes. This sauce can easily dominate a dish, so use sparingly.

This keeps in the fridge for up to three weeks.

**1/2 cup tamari**

**3 tbsp toasted sesame oil**

**1-1/2 inches fresh ginger, peeled and minced**

**4 tbsp lemon juice**

1. Combine all ingredients in a saucepan. Bring to a boil over high heat, reduce heat and simmer 5 minutes.
2. Remove from heat and cool. Serve.

SERVES 6

# ninja 2 sauce

This is the second sauce in the Ninja Rice Bowl (page 61), hence the name. You could use this to perk up any rice, noodle or vegetable dish. Just remember that it is an intensely flavoured sauce and a little goes a long way.

This sauce lasts two weeks in the fridge.

**1/2 cup Simple Sauce (page 106)**
**1-1/2 tsp Hot Sauce (page 105)**

Combine Simple Sauce and Hot Sauce in a bowl and mix well. Serve.

SERVES 8

# pineapple cashew sauce

This sauce is served with the Emerald City noodles (page 80). If you can find only salted cashews at the store, leave the salt out of the sauce, adding it only if necessary. Cashews are a good source of protein and fibre, and are also rich in monounsaturated fats, which are said to help protect the heart.

**3/4 cup raw cashews, unsalted**

**1 clove garlic**

**1/4 cup pineapple juice, fresh or bottled**

**3 tbsp lemon juice**

**1/4 tsp sea salt**

**1/2 cup filtered water**

Combine all ingredients in a blender, and process until smooth. Serve.

SERVES 6

# sesame miso sauce

Jen and her friend Jojo went to Dojo Restaurant in New York City and had a sauce that inspired this one. It is quite strong tasting, so a little goes a long way. It is delicious drizzled on steamed vegetables or rice, or used as we do, in the Big Green noodles (page 79).

**1 cup white wine**
**2 tbsp fresh ginger, minced**
**1/4 cup tahini**
**2 tbsp miso**
**2 tbsp apple cider vinegar**
**1 tbsp tamari**
**1 tsp maple syrup**

1. Combine white wine and ginger in a small pot. Bring to a boil and simmer 3 minutes or until reduced by half. Let cool.
2. Purée white wine mixture, tahini, miso, vinegar, tamari and maple syrup in a blender until smooth. Add a little water if necessary to make it a pourable consistency before serving.

SERVES 6

# coconut curry sauce

This is the sauce used in the Coconut Curry Wrap (page 96). It's also great poured over rice or tossed with noodles and vegetables. In the past few years, many of our customers have asked us to provide wheat-free options. The original Coconut Curry Sauce used wheat flour, but last year, we changed to spelt flour so that those with wheat sensitivities could enjoy this sauce. If you don't have spelt flour on hand, substitute whole wheat, durum or unbleached white flour instead.

**3 tbsp sunflower oil**
**1 small cooking onion, diced**
**2 cloves garlic, minced**
**1/2 tsp cumin, ground**
**3/4 tsp sea salt**

**3 tbsp curry powder**
**3 tbsp light spelt flour**
**2 cups Roasted Vegetable Stock (page 22)**
**2 cups coconut milk**
**3 tomatoes, diced**

1. Heat oil in a pot over medium heat.
2. Add onion and garlic; cook 5 minutes until softened.
3. Add cumin, salt and curry powder; cook for 1 minute.
4. Add flour and cook for 1 minute, stirring frequently.
5. Stir in the Roasted Vegetable Stock gradually to prevent lumps from forming.
6. Add the coconut milk and tomatoes.
7. Bring to a boil, stirring occasionally. Simmer for 20 to 30 minutes until slightly thickened. Serve.

SERVES 6

# rich mushroom sauce

This sauce is served over the Southwestern Polenta (page 145). You can leave the chipotle peppers out if you prefer a more traditional Italian flavour. Any one or a combination of button, shiitake, portobello or oyster mushrooms will work well in this recipe.

4 tbsp olive oil

4 cloves garlic, minced

12 cups mushrooms, sliced

1-1/2 tsp dried thyme

1/2 tsp dried rosemary

2 cups crushed tomatoes, canned

2/3 cup white wine

6 tbsp balsamic vinegar

2 tbsp adobo sauce (from the chipotles in
    the Southwestern Polenta recipe, page 145)

4 tbsp fresh parsley, chopped

1/4 tsp sea salt

1/4 tsp black pepper

1.  Heat oil in a pot over medium heat.
2.  Sauté garlic in olive oil for 1 minute, being careful not to let it burn.
3.  Add mushrooms, thyme and rosemary.
4.  Cook 5 minutes, until mushrooms start to release their liquid.
5.  Add crushed tomatoes, white wine, balsamic vinegar and adobo sauce.
6.  Simmer 30 minutes, then add parsley, salt and pepper. Serve.

SERVES 4

# bbq sauce

This is the sauce we use in the BBQ Tempeh Wrap (page 89). It also makes a nice glaze for baked tofu or grilled portobello mushrooms. This sauce will keep for two weeks in the fridge.

| | |
|---|---|
| 4 tbsp olive oil | 3/4 cup apple cider vinegar |
| 1 onion, diced | 3/4 cup filtered water |
| 2 cloves garlic | 3/4 cup natural ketchup |
| 2 tsp allspice | 4 tsp sesame oil |
| 1 tsp cayenne | 3 tbsp Bragg's Liquid Aminos or tamari |
| 1/2 cup raw, unrefined sugar | 3 tbsp molasses |

1. Heat oil in a saucepan over medium low heat.
2. Add onion, garlic, allspice and cayenne. Sauté 5 minutes until onion is softened.
3. Add remaining ingredients. Bring to a boil and reduce heat.
4. Simmer 30 minutes, until thickened. Serve.

SERVES 6

# special sauce

This sauce goes on The Big Zim sandwich (page 91) but would be tasty on any kind of veggie burger or wrap. It tastes just like the ubiquitous "special sauce" found in fast-food joints the world over.

**2/3 cup Honey Mustard Mayo (page 123)**
**1/3 cup natural ketchup**

Combine Honey Mustard Mayo and ketchup in a bowl; mix well. Serve.

SERVES 4–6

# adzuki bean stew

The Japanese adzuki bean is a tasty small red bean packed with nutrition. It contains 25 percent protein and is high in soluble fibre, which helps to eliminate cholesterol from the body. This bean is also a good source of magnesium, potassium, iron, zinc, copper, manganese and vitamin B3. Because it is high in potassium and low in sodium, it is said to help reduce blood pressure. The red adzuki bean also contains protease inhibitors, reputed to stall development of cancer cells. All this and it tastes great!

This hearty stew is delicious with a simple bowl of brown rice, a dash of Tahini Sauce (page 52) and sliced cucumber or avocado. At Fresh we serve it in the Gospel Rice Bowl (page 71) and the Adzuki Wrap (page 97).

This stew keeps in the fridge for up to five days. It also freezes nicely. If you use this stew in a wrap, decrease the amount of water. Adzuki beans are available dried or canned at some supermarkets and at most health food stores.

| | |
|---|---|
| **4 tbsp olive oil** | **1/4 tsp ground cinnamon** |
| **2 cooking onions, diced** | **4 cups cooked or canned adzuki beans** |
| **2 tbsp fresh ginger, minced** | **2 tbsp tomato paste** |
| **2 tsp dried oregano** | **1/4 cup tamari** |
| **1 tsp cayenne pepper** | **2 cups Roasted Vegetable Stock (page 22)** |

1. Heat oil in a pot over medium heat.
2. Add onions and ginger; cook 5 minutes until softened.
3. Add oregano, cayenne and cinnamon. Stir and cook for 1 minute.
4. Add beans, tomato paste, tamari and Roasted Vegetable Stock.
5. Bring to a boil and simmer for 10 minutes. Serve.

SERVES 4

# black bean mix

This is a side dish to the Nuevos Rancheros (page 141). This mix also makes a great burrito filling.

**6 tbsp olive oil**

**2 onions, chopped**

**4 cloves garlic, minced**

**2 tsp cumin seeds, toasted and ground**

**1 tsp cayenne pepper**

**2 tsp apple cider vinegar**

**1 tsp sea salt**

**4 cups cooked or canned black beans**

1. Heat oil in a pan over medium-high heat.
2. Add onions and sauté until lightly browned.
3. Add garlic, cumin, cayenne, vinegar and salt. Simmer for 5 minutes.
4. Roughly mash black beans by hand or in a food processor.
5. Add black beans to onion mixture, stir and cook 2 minutes, until heated through. Serve.

SERVES 6

# falafel ball mix

Falafel is a tasty, nutritious, high-protein food that is inexpensive and very filling. At the restaurant we serve the falafel balls as an appetizer called the Middle Eastern Plate, with hummus, flax pita, tomato slices, parsley and kalamata olives. For a great meal on the go, check out the Falafel in a Pita (page 99).

| | |
|---|---|
| 2 cups cooked or canned chickpeas | 1 tsp cumin, toasted and ground |
| 1/4 cup dried bulgur | 1/3 cup tahini |
| 1 tbsp filtered water | 1 tsp turmeric |
| 4 cloves garlic | 1/2 tsp coriander, toasted and ground |
| 1 red onion, chopped | 1/4 tsp cayenne pepper |
| 1/2 cup parsley, chopped | 1/3 cup bread crumbs |
| 2 green onions, chopped | 1/3 cup whole wheat flour |
| 1/4 tsp sea salt | 1/4 cup canola oil |

1. Spread chickpeas on a cookie sheet and let dry for 1 hour.
2. Put bulgur in a small bowl and add the water. Mix and set aside.
3. In a food processor, finely mince the garlic, red onion, parsley and green onions. Place in a large mixing bowl.
4. Purée chickpeas in the food processor. Add to garlic mixture.
5. Add salt, cumin, tahini, turmeric, coriander, cayenne, bread crumbs, whole wheat flour and bulgur. Mix thoroughly.
6. Roll the mix between the palms of your hands to form 1-inch balls. Sauté falafel balls in oil 2 minutes per side until golden and crispy. Serve.

MAKES 24

# spreads, coatings and marinades

If rice, noodles, sauces and vegetables form the basis of our menu, this section provides the exciting flavour punches that take a meal from ordinary to fabulous.

Our spreads give that certain je ne sais quoi to a sandwich or wrap without resorting to plain old mayos or margarines. Some of our spreads are vegan versions of familiar dairy products, such as the Tofu Whip (page 122), Tofu Sour Cream (page 120) and Savoury Tofu Ricotta (page 121). You will soon realize that you don't have to give up the creamy goodness of these products just because you don't eat dairy.

The Crispy Tofu Coating (page 130) has become almost legendary in its allure, with customers repeatedly asking for the recipe ever since the coating first appeared in our specials.
It can be used to bread almost anything, or even be sprinkled on top of noodles or pasta as a substitute for Parmesan.

Certain foods really need help to prevent them from tasting bland and boring. This is where our marinades come in. Tofu, tempeh and sea vegetables absorb whatever flavours you soak them in, so don't be limited by our suggestions. Add your favourite flavourings. Not into basil and marjoram? Then substitute Herbes de Provence for our Mixed Herbs. Don't like licorice? Then use coriander instead of anise in the tempeh marinade. Once you've mastered our basic recipes, follow your taste buds. You never know when you'll come up with a new favourite flavour combination.

# tofu sour cream

This sour cream can be used wherever you would normally use the dairy version. A dollop of it goes great over a bowl of Mushroom Stroganoff Soup (page 34).

Depending on the water content of the tofu you are using, you may have to add a bit of water to get a sour cream–like consistency. Be patient: it may take a few minutes to achieve a really smooth sour cream. The tofu will go through a grainy stage, but keep processing and it will become velvety smooth, just like the real thing.

If you are keeping this in the fridge, it may solidify. You can either whiz it up again in the food processor with a bit of water, or just stir it vigorously until it loosens up. It keeps in the fridge for about three days.

**2 cups firm tofu, chopped**
**3 tbsp sunflower oil**
**3 tbsp + 1 tsp lemon juice**
**1 tbsp raw, unrefined sugar**
**1/2 tsp sea salt**

Process all ingredients in a food processor until smooth, scraping down the sides of the bowl periodically.

SERVES 8

# savoury tofu ricotta

Neither of us likes processed soy cheeses; they taste and feel like nothing that exists in nature. We really wanted to make a cheese substitute that would be good on our pizzas, and this is it. It tastes just like real ricotta and you can use it wherever you would use the real thing.

**2 cloves garlic**
**2 cups firm tofu, chopped**
**3 tbsp olive oil**
**2 tbsp lemon juice**
**1/2 tsp sea salt**
**1 tsp miso**
**1/4 tsp dried rosemary**

1. In a food processor, mince the garlic.
2. Add tofu, oil, lemon juice, salt, miso and rosemary.
3. Process, using the pulse button. Stop and scrape the sides of the food processor periodically. The mixture shouldn't be totally smooth, but more lumpy or granular, like real ricotta.

SERVES 8

# tofu whip

This is a great substitute for whipped cream and is delicious on waffles, pancakes or crepes. At Fresh, the Tofu Whip is served on a bowl of maple walnut granola with fresh berries and rice milk. It is also a great accompaniment to the Banana Walnut Polenta (page 151). Be sure to process for a long time, to get a perfectly smooth consistency. It keeps for two or three days in the fridge.

**2 cups firm tofu, chopped**
**1 tsp vanilla extract**
**3 tbsp honey**
**1/4 tsp sea salt**
**1/2 cup vanilla soymilk**

Process all ingredients in a food processor until smooth, scraping down the sides of the bowl periodically.

SERVES 8

# honey mustard mayo

We adore this mayo and can't seem to stop ourselves from using it everywhere. You will find it appears in many of our sandwiches, like the BBQ Tempeh Wrap (page 89), Magic Tofu Sandwich (page 90), Soho Sandwich (page 92), Wrapper's Delight (page 93), Voodoo Sandwich (page 94) and Bermuda Triangle (page 95). Keeps up to four days in the fridge.

| | |
|---|---|
| 1/2 onion, chopped | 4 tbsp filtered water |
| 1 clove garlic, minced | 2 tsp miso |
| 2 tsp white wine | 1 cup firm tofu, chopped |
| Pinch sea salt | 2 tsp Dijon mustard |
| Pinch nutmeg | 2 tbsp honey |
| Pinch black pepper | 3 tbsp sunflower oil |
| 1/4 tsp Mixed Herbs (page 124) | 2 tsp apple cider vinegar |

1.  Boil onion, garlic, white wine, salt, nutmeg, pepper, Mixed Herbs and water in a pan over medium heat for 2 to 5 minutes until liquid has evaporated. Stir occasionally and be careful not to let it burn. Cool.
2.  In a food processor, process onion mixture and remaining ingredients until smooth.

SERVES 4–6

# mixed herbs

This combination of dried herbs adds flavour to many of our recipes. The mixture will last forever; just give it a little rub between your fingers before using to release the flavours and aromas. Mixed Herbs are great sprinkled on salads, pastas, noodles or rice bowls. Keeps indefinitely in a sealed jar.

**1 tbsp dried oregano**

**1 tbsp dried basil**

**1 tbsp dried marjoram**

**1 tbsp dried dill**

**1 tbsp dried thyme**

**1-1/2 tsp dried rosemary**

**1-1/2 tsp dried sage**

Combine all ingredients in a bowl. Mix well.

MAKES 6 TABLESPOONS

# hummus

This is our basic hummus recipe. It can be adjusted in countless ways, depending on your preference. You could add parsley or cilantro for an herbal twist, some toasted cumin and cayenne for a bit of spice, or some roasted red peppers, black olives or sun-dried tomatoes for a Mediterranean taste. If you prefer a milder garlic flavour, roast the garlic before using.

**2 cups cooked or canned chickpeas**
**3 cloves garlic**
**2 tbsp tahini**
**4 tbsp lemon juice**
**1/2 tsp sea salt**
**1 tbsp filtered water**

In a food processor, purée all ingredients. Add more water if necessary to get the consistency you like.

SERVES 8

# harissa

This spicy exotic paste is jammed with flavour and heat. Use it in the Peace and Love Salad (page 42) or spread it in the Falafel in a Pita (page 99). This sauce will last a couple of weeks in the fridge.

**1 tsp caraway seeds**
**1 tsp cumin seeds**
**1 tsp coriander seeds**
**Pinch sea salt**
**3 tbsp paprika**
**1 tbsp red chili flakes**
**2 cloves garlic, minced**
**1 tbsp olive oil**

1. Toast the caraway, cumin and coriander seeds in a dry skillet over medium heat, about 3 minutes or until slightly brown and fragrant. Let cool.
2. Grind the seeds in a spice grinder or with a mortar and pestle. Add salt and grind again.
3. Add paprika and chili flakes; grind again.
4. Transfer to a mixing bowl. Add garlic and olive oil; mix well.

SERVES 8

# pesto

Contrary to popular belief, you don't need Parmesan to make a delicious pesto. Our version is packed with flavour and is a bit different from the classic because of the addition of fresh spinach and sunflower seeds. These ingredients add colour and taste, and save money. (Pine nuts are great but can really break the bank!) Store Pesto in the fridge (for two weeks) or in the freezer. A dollop of Pesto is added to the Sicilian White Bean and Tomato Soup (page 24), and it can also be used as a topping for pasta or pizza, as a sandwich spread or even tossed with grilled vegetables for a warm salad.

**2 cloves garlic, minced**
**1 tsp sea salt**
**1/4 cup sunflower seeds, raw and unsalted**
**1/3 cup pine nuts**
**3 tbsp olive oil**
**1 bunch fresh basil, stems removed**
**2 cups chopped fresh spinach**

1. Process garlic, salt, sunflower seeds, pine nuts and olive oil in a food processor until finely minced.
2. Add the basil and spinach and process until smooth, scraping the sides down periodically.

SERVES 8

# herb tofu mayo

This was our first successful mayo ever. It has a permanent place on our menu in several signature dishes, including our veggie burgers. In this cookbook, it appears in the Reality Bites sandwich (page 88). This will last up to five days in the fridge.

**2 cups firm tofu, chopped**

**1 clove garlic, minced**

**1 tbsp apple cider vinegar**

**1 tsp Dijon mustard**

**1 tsp sea salt**

**1/2 tsp ground white pepper**

**1/4 cup filtered water**

**1 tbsp sunflower oil**

**3 tbsp Mixed Herbs (page 124)**

1. In a food processor, process the tofu, garlic and vinegar until smooth, scraping down sides periodically.
2. Add mustard, salt, pepper, water, oil and Mixed Herbs; process until smooth.

SERVES 8

# chickpea spread

This mixture goes in the Power Lunch sandwich (page 98), but would be equally at home in a wrap or served on a bed of greens.

**1-3/4 cups cooked or canned chickpeas**
**1 cup grated carrots**
**1 stalk celery, finely chopped**
**1 green onion, finely chopped**
**1 tbsp Dijon mustard**
**1 large dill pickle, finely chopped**
**2 tbsp Honey Mustard Mayo (page 123)**
**1 tsp lemon juice**
**Pinch sea salt**

1. Break up the cooked chickpeas coarsely, using a food processor or a potato masher.
2. Combine chickpeas, carrots, celery, onion, mustard, pickle, Honey Mustard Mayo, lemon juice and salt in a large bowl. Mix well.

SERVES 4

# crispy tofu coating

Ever since we put Crispy Tofu on the menu, people have been calling to ask for the recipe. We have kept secret until now how utterly simple it really is!

Crispy tofu cubes and steaks are a great way to get people who think they don't like tofu to try it. It has a certain down-home southern-fried taste that appeals to meat eaters and vegetarians alike.

This dry mix lasts indefinitely, as long as it doesn't have chunks of tofu or food left in it. It's a good idea to remove the amount of coating you need, so that if little bits of food break off, you haven't contaminated the whole batch. At Fresh, we use it to coat Marinated Tofu Cubes (page 132) in the Ninja Rice Bowl (page 61), Marinated Tofu Steaks (page 133) in the Magic Tofu Sandwich (page 90) and eggplant in The Big Zim (page 91).

**1 cup flaked nutritional yeast**
**1/2 cup wheat germ**
**1 tbsp garlic powder**
**1/4 tsp sea salt**
**1/4 tsp black pepper**

Combine all ingredients in a bowl; mix.

SERVES 6

# marinated tempeh

Tempeh is generally sold frozen in blocks. To prepare it for marinating, remove the wrapping and drop it into a shallow pan of boiling water. Remove the tempeh once it is soft. This should only take a couple of minutes. Let it cool, then cut it in 1/4-inch slices. Stored in a sealed container in the fridge, marinated tempeh keeps for up to a week.

Marinated tempeh is used in the Wildfire Noodles (page 77), Satori Noodles (page 82), Revival Rice Bowl (page 62) and BBQ Tempeh Wrap (page 89).

**2 tbsp filtered water**

**2 tsp honey**

**1/3 cup tamari**

**1/3 cup balsamic vinegar**

**1 tbsp sesame oil**

**1 tbsp sunflower oil**

**1 tsp white pepper**

**1-1/2 tsp ground anise**

**2 tsp garlic powder**

**1 block tempeh**

1. Mix all ingredients, except tempeh, in a bowl.
2. Pour marinade over tempeh.
3. Marinate for at least 1 hour.

SERVES 4

# marinated tofu cubes

When making this marinade, it is very important to mix the ingredients first, before pouring them over the tofu. If you pour the individual ingredients over the tofu, whatever you put in first will be the only thing that flavours the tofu.

At our restaurants, we cut a regular-size block of tofu into 64 cubes (4 × 4 × 4), to ensure that each cube has plenty of flavour. Because a marinade will penetrate only a couple of millimetres into the tofu, the cubes should be small enough so there is not too much plain tofu left in the middle of each.

There is enough marinade in this recipe to cover two blocks of firm tofu. Stored in a sealed container in the fridge, the cubes will keep for up to three days.

These cubes are used in the New Buddha Rice Bowl (page 60), the Ninja Rice Bowl (page 61), the Wrapper's Delight (page 93), The Raw Truth Salad (page 38) and The Bohemian Salad (page 45).

**1/2 cup apple cider vinegar**
**3/4 cup tamari**
**1/4 cup filtered water**
**1-1/2 tbsp sunflower oil**
**1 9 oz (250 g) block firm tofu, cut into 64 cubes**

1. Mix vinegar, tamari, water and oil thoroughly in a large bowl. Pour marinade over tofu cubes.
2. Marinate cubes for at least 15 minutes.

MAKES 64 CUBES

# marinated tofu steaks

Stored in a sealed container in the fridge, these steaks keep up to three days. Marinated Tofu Steaks are sublime in the Green Destiny Salad (page 39), Samurai Soba (page 76), Big Green Noodles (page 79), Sunflower Rice Bowl (page 67), Hijiki Rice Bowl (page 68), Power House Rice Bowl (page 70) and Magic Tofu Sandwich (page 90).

**1 9 oz (250 g) block firm tofu**
**2 tbsp coriander, ground**
**4 tsp garlic powder**
**1/2 cup tamari**
**2 cups filtered water**

1. Cut the block of tofu into 4-1/4-inch thick slices, then cut the slices diagonally into triangles.
2. Combine the coriander, garlic, tamari and water in a bowl; mix well. Pour marinade over tofu triangles.
3. Marinate for at least 1 hour.

MAKES 8

# marinated aramé and hijiki

Aramé and hijiki are sold in dried form either packaged or in bulk. To prepare for use, first reconstitute these sea vegetables in filtered water. Be careful not to let them soak for longer than 20 minutes or all the goodness will go into the water and then down the drain. Stored in a sealed container in the fridge, these keep for up to five days.

**1/2 cup dry aramé or hijiki**
**2 cups filtered water**
**1/8 batch Simple Sauce (page 106)**

1. Place aramé or hijiki in a medium-sized bowl. Add room-temperature water to cover by about 3 inches. Soak for 15 minutes or until expanded and soft. Drain.
2. Add Simple Sauce and marinate for at least 1 hour.

SERVES 4

# marinated sun-dried tomatoes

These tomatoes keep at least a week in the fridge as long as they are covered with olive oil. Once you have finished using the sun-dried tomatoes, use the flavoured oil for cooking or salad dressing.

**3 cups filtered water**
**1 cup sun-dried tomatoes**
**3/4 cup olive oil**
**1 tbsp Mixed Herbs (page 124)**

1. Bring water to a boil in a pot.
2. Add sun-dried tomatoes and remove from heat.
3. Let sit until tomatoes are tender, about 10 to 20 minutes. Drain.
4. Mix olive oil and Mixed Herbs; pour over tomatoes.

SERVES 4

Weekend brunch at the Fresh restaurants is always busy, fun and a little bit crazy.

The day is full of promise as staff arrive early to fill the sugar, maple syrup, ketchup and hot sauce containers, to list brunch items on the specials boards, and to make sure they have enough cutlery roll-ups for the day.

Customers arrive hungry for a hearty breakfast and revitalizing fresh juice and reward themselves for finally making it to the weekend. Sweet and savoury cooking smells waft from the open kitchens, bringing hints of the good food to come. The dining rooms are noisy with the hum of juicers, blenders and the busy espresso machine, while great music from all over the world competes to be heard.

Weekend brunch means not having to worry about going back to the office when all you really want to do is go back to bed. Brunch is about indulging in yummy comfort foods that make us feel satiated, without resorting to the use of old standards like eggs, cheese, cream and butter.

# brunch

# scrambled tofu

We've tried lots of versions of scrambled tofu over the years, and this one is our favourite. Scrambled tofu can be used in wraps, on toast, on English muffins or anywhere else that you would use eggs. We like it in the Spinach Tofu Wrap (page 139), Green Eggs (page 140) and Nuevos Rancheros (page 141). We're sure that after you try it, you will develop your own favourite recipes to enjoy it.

We make the seasonings into a paste so the flavour will travel throughout the tofu.

This mixture will keep in the fridge for up to three days. To reheat, add a little water and warm in a skillet over medium heat until water has evaporated.

| | |
|---|---|
| 2 tbsp olive oil | 1/2 tsp sea salt |
| 1 onion, finely diced | 1/2 tsp black pepper |
| 1 clove garlic, minced | Pinch turmeric |
| 1 tbsp Engevita yeast | 1/4 cup filtered water |
| 3/4 tsp dillweed | 2 cups chopped firm tofu |
| 1 tsp garlic powder | |

1. Heat oil in a pot over medium heat.
2. Add onion and garlic; cook 5 minutes or until soft, stirring often.
3. Mix Engevita yeast, dillweed, garlic powder, salt, black pepper, turmeric and water in a small bowl.
4. Crumble tofu and add to onion mixture. Stir.
5. Add yeast mixture and stir 1 minute or until thoroughly heated and most of liquid has evaporated. Serve.

SERVES 2

# spinach tofu wrap

This is one of our most popular breakfast specials. It is also very good with alfalfa sprouts inside.

**2 tbsp olive oil**

**1 tomato, chopped**

**1 cup grated carrot**

**2 cups fresh spinach, chopped**

**1/2 batch Scrambled Tofu (page 138)**

**1 tbsp filtered water**

**2 10-inch spinach tortillas**

**4 tbsp Honey Mustard Mayo (page 123)**

1. Heat oil in a skillet over medium heat.
2. Add tomato, carrot and spinach; cook 1 minute until softened.
3. Add Scrambled Tofu and water. Cook 1 minute or until heated through and water evaporates.
4. Meanwhile, warm tortillas for 2 minutes in a 350°F oven. Spread with Honey Mustard Mayo.
5. Divide tofu mixture between the tortillas and roll up. Serve.

SERVES 2

# green eggs

This scrambled tofu mixture is great served with toast, sliced tomato (either raw or grilled), Home Fries (page 143), baked beans and vegan sausages or bacon. We use Yves brand vegan sausages and bacon, which taste almost like the real thing.

**2 tbsp olive oil**
**1/2 red pepper, chopped**
**1/2 green pepper, chopped**
**1 cup sliced button mushrooms**
**1 batch Scrambled Tofu (page 138)**
**1 tbsp filtered water**

1. Heat oil in a skillet over medium heat.
2. Add red and green pepper and mushrooms. Cook 5 minutes or until mushrooms are browned.
3. Add Scrambled Tofu and water. Cook 1 minute or until heated through. Serve.

SERVES 2

# nuevos rancheros

Add some spice to your mornings with our version of this classic Mexican dish. It is an unusual breakfast, perfect for those days when you feel like something a little different.

1/4 cup + 1 tbsp olive oil

4 corn tortillas

Pinch sea salt

1/2 batch Black Bean Mix (page 115)

2 tomatoes, chopped

1 jalapeno pepper, minced

1 batch Scrambled Tofu (page 138)

1 tbsp filtered water

1/2 avocado, sliced

2 green onions, finely sliced

1. Heat 1/4 cup oil in a pan over medium heat. Add corn tortillas and fry until crisp. (You may have to do this one at a time, depending on the size of your pan.) Sprinkle with salt, drain on paper towels and set aside.

2. In a saucepan over medium heat, warm Black Bean Mix, stirring often. Set aside.

3. In a skillet, heat remaining 1 tablespoon oil. Add tomatoes and jalapeno; cook until softened.

4. Add Scrambled Tofu and water. Cook 1 minute or until heated through.

5. Put 2 tortillas on each plate and top with Scrambled Tofu. Spoon Black Bean Mix on the side. Garnish with avocado slices and green onions.

SERVES 2

# gallo pinto

This Costa Rican specialty is a great brunch item, especially when served with a green salad and some sliced avocado. Serve with Lizano, a traditional Costa Rican condiment or substitute HP Sauce.

| | |
|---|---|
| 1 cup dry black beans | 1-1/2 cups onion, chopped |
| 2 cloves garlic, whole | 2 cloves garlic, minced |
| 1-1/2 tsp oregano, dry | 2 tbsp tamari |
| 1/2 cup fresh cilantro, chopped | 1/2 tsp sea salt |
| 9 cups filtered water | 3 cups cooked brown basmati rice |
| 1 tbsp olive oil | |

1. Bring beans, whole garlic cloves, oregano, cilantro and water to a boil. Cook 1-1/2 to 2 hours, or until beans are tender.
2. Drain beans and remove and discard garlic cloves.
3. In a saucepan, heat oil. Add onions and minced garlic and cook 5 minutes or until softened. Add tamari and salt. Stir.
4. Add black bean mixture to the pan, mashing beans slightly to mix with the onions.
5. Add cooked basmati rice to the pan and mix thoroughly until everything is hot, about 2 minutes. Serve.

SERVES 4

# home fries

The secret to great home fries is blanching (boiling) them first. Shaking the potatoes around in the pot breaks up the edges and creates lots of little nooks and crannies that get nice and crispy. If you want your home fries to be a little spicy, substitute Cajun seasoning for the Mixed Herbs.

**8 cups water**
**2 potatoes, chopped into bite-sized pieces**
**2 tbsp olive oil**
**1 tsp Mixed Herbs (page 124)**
**1 clove garlic, minced (optional)**
**1/2 tsp sea salt**

1. Bring water to a boil in a saucepan and add potatoes.
2. Reduce heat and simmer 10 to 15 minutes or until potatoes are almost tender.
3. Drain potatoes, return them to the pot and shake them around a bit to roughen up the edges.
4. Toss potatoes with oil, Mixed Herbs and garlic (if using). Spread on baking sheet.
5. Bake in 400°F oven until crispy, about 15 to 20 minutes.
6. Remove from oven and sprinkle with salt. Serve.

SERVES 2

# potato cakes

We serve these with Tofu Sour Cream (page 120) and a side salad. Ketchup, salsa or HP Sauce are great accompaniments too.

**2 potatoes, peeled and grated**
**4 tbsp cilantro, minced**
**1/4 red pepper, minced**
**1/4 red onion, minced**
**1/2 tsp sea salt**
**1/4 tsp black pepper**
**1/4 cup olive oil**

1. Mix potatoes, cilantro, red pepper, onion, salt and black pepper in a bowl.
2. Heat oil in a skillet over medium heat.
3. Form potato mixture into 4 patties and gently place in a pan. You may have to do 2 at a time, depending on the size of your pan. Cook 10 minutes, turning after 5 minutes, until potatoes are soft and browned. (Do not disturb them too much or they will break apart.)

SERVES 2

# southwestern polenta

The secret to making good polenta is cooking it long enough. When you make it, you will see that about a minute after you add the cornmeal to the water, it gets really thick and looks as if it's done. But don't be fooled. If you stop cooking it then, it will be all grainy and raw tasting. You need to cook it for about 40 minutes, and you will see that the colour lightens, and each grain of cornmeal softens, so that the whole thing is beautifully smooth. Just remember to cook it over really low heat, or you'll get a lava-like explosion of polenta all over your kitchen!

You can eat this polenta soft, right out of the pot, with the sauce and whatever accompaniment you want, or as described in this recipe. Both ways are delicious.

Chipotles are smoked jalapenos and give this dish a really distinctive flavour. They are available at specialty food stores, usually in small cans, and usually they have been packed in an adobo sauce. Both the peppers and the sauce freeze well, so there's no need to waste the leftovers. Add a little of the chipotles the next time you're making chili for an authentic Tex-Mex taste.

If you prefer a more traditional, Italian flavour for this dish, leave the corn and chipotles out.

Serve the polenta and sauce with some steamed greens or spinach, a leafy salad or any type of vegetable.

**6 cups water**
**1 tbsp sea salt**
**1-1/2 cups yellow cornmeal**
**1/2 cup corn niblets**
**3 chipotles, chopped**
**1 batch Rich Mushroom Sauce (page 111)**

1. Bring water and salt to a boil in a large saucepan.
2. Pour cornmeal into the water in a stream, while stirring. Bring to a boil, stirring constantly, then turn heat down to very low. Cook for 35 minutes, stirring occasionally.
3. Stir in corn and chipotles; cook for 5 minutes.
4. Spread polenta into a half-inch-thick rectangle on an oiled baking sheet, getting it as smooth as you can.
5. Cover with plastic wrap and refrigerate approximately 30 minutes, until the polenta hardens.

6. Cut polenta into 8 squares or triangles.

7. Warm Rich Mushroom Sauce in a saucepan over medium heat, stirring often.

8. To heat the polenta, bake, grill or sauté it:

   - To bake, brush polenta with 1 tablespoon oil. Bake on a baking sheet at 400°F for 10 to 15 minutes or until heated through.

   - To grill, brush polenta with oil, then grill both sides (about 5 minutes per side).

   - To sauté, heat 1 tablespoon of oil in a skillet over medium heat. Add polenta, cooking until heated through (about 5 minutes per side).

9. Put polenta on plates and cover with the warm Rich Mushroom Sauce.

SERVES 4

# orange spelt crepes

We use this batter for our Dolce Vita special (page 150), but you could fill these crepes with fruit, Tofu Whip (page 122) or even just some lemon juice and sugar, like Jen's grandfather used to make for her and her sister every spring on Pancake Tuesday.

This recipe makes eight crepes, with a little batter left over for mistakes, because, as anyone who has ever made crepes knows, the first one never works out.

**1-3/4 cups spelt flour**
**1/2 tsp baking soda**
**1/2 tsp baking powder**
**1/2 tsp orange zest (page 9)**
**1/2 tsp orange juice**

**1 tbsp honey**
**2 tbsp maple syrup**
**2/3 cup vanilla soymilk**
**1-1/4 cups filtered water**
**8 tsp sunflower oil**

1. Mix flour, baking soda, baking powder and zest in a bowl.
2. Mix orange juice, honey, maple syrup, soymilk and water in a pitcher.
3. Add dry ingredients to wet, and whisk until smooth.
4. Heat 1 teaspoon oil in a crepe pan over medium-low heat and add just enough crepe batter to thinly cover bottom (1/8 of the batter). Cook until batter is set. Flip over and cook a few seconds more.
5. Remove from the pan and set aside in a 250°F oven until ready to use. Repeat for remaining 7 crepes.

SERVES 4

# sweet tofu ricotta

This mix is used as the filling for our Dolce Vita crepes (page 150). It will keep for a couple of days in the fridge. If you have any left over, purée it until smooth and use it as a whipped cream substitute.

**2 cups chopped firm tofu**
**1 tbsp vanilla extract**
**3 tbsp honey**
**2 tbsp vanilla soymilk**

Pulse all ingredients several times in food processor until they reach a ricotta consistency.

SERVES 4

# candied pecans

We use these delicious pecans in our Dolce Vita crepes (page 150), but they are great on their own as a snack, on top of granola or even tossed in a salad. They will last at least a week, but we bet you won't have them around that long. Substitute cashews, walnuts, hazelnuts, almonds or a mixture.

**1/2 cup raw, unrefined sugar**
**4 tsp filtered water**
**1 cup pecan halves, toasted**
**1/4 tsp canola oil**

1. Heat sugar and water in a pot over medium heat, stirring, for 5 minutes or until sugar is dissolved.
2. Add pecans and stir.
3. Oil a baking sheet and spread pecans on it. When hardened, break clusters and store in a sealed container.

SERVES 4

# dolce vita

Theresa DeGrace, a former kitchen manager at Bloor Street, came up with this popular wheat-free breakfast special, which has many loyal fans. These crepes use Sweet Tofu Ricotta as a filling, which is set off perfectly by the Candied Pecans. You can substitute any other kinds of nuts, but we are partial to pecans. Serve these crepes with fresh fruit salad and pure maple syrup.

To make the crepes, it really helps to have a crepe pan or non-stick skillet.

**1 batch Sweet Tofu Ricotta (page 148)**
**1 batch Orange Spelt Crepes, warm (page 147)**
**1 batch Candied Pecans (page 149)**

1. Spread 1/8 of the Sweet Tofu Ricotta over each crepe and sprinkle each with 1/8 of the Candied Pecans.
2. Roll up and serve.

SERVES 4

# banana walnut polenta

This is a great breakfast entrée. It is unusual enough to do for a special brunch, but easy enough that you will be able to spend time with your guests. You can cook the polenta the day before and keep it in the fridge until you are ready to reheat it. Serve with fruit salad or sliced berries.

For tips on cooking polenta, see Southwestern Polenta (page 145).

| | | |
|---|---|---|
| 6 cups water | 1 tsp ground cinnamon | 8 tbsp maple syrup |
| 1-1/2 cups yellow cornmeal | 4 tbsp sunflower oil | 1 cup chopped walnuts, toasted |
| 2 tbsp raw, unrefined sugar | 4 bananas, sliced | 1 batch Tofu Whip (page 122) |

1. Bring water to a boil.
2. Mix cornmeal, sugar and cinnamon in a bowl.
3. Pour cornmeal mixture into the water in a stream while stirring. Bring to a boil, stirring constantly, then turn heat down to very low. Cook for 40 minutes, stirring occasionally.
4. Spread polenta into a half-inch-thick rectangle on an oiled baking sheet, getting it as smooth as you can.
5. Cover with plastic wrap and refrigerate approximately 30 minutes, until the polenta hardens.
6. Cut polenta into 8 squares or triangles.
7. To heat the polenta, bake, grill or sauté it, then keep warm in a 250°F oven:
   - To bake, brush polenta with 1 tablespoon oil. Bake on a baking sheet at 400°F for 10 to 15 minutes or until heated through.
   - To grill, brush polenta with oil, then grill both sides (about 5 minutes per side).
   - To sauté, heat 1 tablespoon of oil in a skillet over medium heat. Add polenta, cooking until heated through (about 5 minutes per side).
8. Heat oil in a skillet over medium heat. Add sliced bananas and cook 2 minutes until browned. Add maple syrup and walnuts. Cook 1 minute or until heated through.
9. Put polenta onto plates.
10. Pour banana mixture over polenta and top with Tofu Whip. Serve.

SERVES 4

# tofu omelette

This omelette appears in the Shinto Rice Bowl (page 72) and the Spring Omelette (page 153). The amount of gluten flour required will vary, depending on the day. If you have time, let the mixture sit for a couple of hours in the fridge to make it easier to roll out.

| | |
|---|---|
| 2 tbsp olive oil | 1-1/2 tbsp Engevita yeast |
| 1/2 onion, sliced | 1/2 cup gluten flour |
| 1/2 cup carrot, grated | 1-1/2 tsp sea salt |
| 1/2 cup chopped green onions | 1-1/2 tsp black pepper |
| 3 cloves garlic | 4 tbsp whole wheat flour |
| 3-1/2 cups firm tofu, chopped | 2 tbsp sunflower oil |

1. Heat olive oil in a skillet over medium heat. Add onion and cook 5 minutes or until onion is browned. Let cool.
2. Put onion, carrot, green onions and garlic into the bowl of a food processor. Process until finely minced.
3. Add tofu and process with other ingredients until thoroughly mixed.
4. Add Engevita yeast, gluten flour, salt and pepper. Mixture should be firm and easy to handle. If it is sticky, add some more gluten flour and process until combined.
5. Sprinkle the whole wheat flour over a flat surface. Roll out 1/6 of the mixture to a 6-inch circle, 1/4 inch thick. Repeat for each omelette.
6. In a large skillet, heat sunflower oil. Cook omelettes about 6 minutes until brown on both sides. If necessary, keep omelettes warm in a 250ºF oven while cooking others. Serve.

SERVES 6

# spring omelette

Yasi, our former kitchen manager at the Crawford location, invented this brunch option. She made it for herself one day and was so impressed that she immediately made herself another one, and then turned it into a special. In the spring, try adding asparagus. Arugula or baby spinach would also be wonderful inside this fluffy omelette.

**1 batch Tofu Omelette (page 152)**
**4 tbsp olive oil**
**6 cups mushrooms, sliced**
**1 cup red onion, sliced**
**3 tomatoes, chopped**
**4 tbsp Mixed Herbs (page 124)**
**1 batch Savoury Tofu Ricotta (page 121)**

1. Prepare omelettes and keep warm in a 250°F oven.
2. In a skillet, heat the oil. Add mushrooms, onion and tomatoes. Cook 5 minutes or until mushrooms are browned. Add Mixed Herbs and stir.
3. Spread each omelette with Tofu Ricotta and top with cooked vegetables. Fold over and serve.

SERVES 6

# desserts

Back in the first few years of operating our Bloor Street location, we did all our own baking. We had a huge, ancient convection oven with doors that opened so wide that all action in the kitchen came to a screeching halt every time someone put something in or took something out. As Bloor got busier, baking became more and more of a nuisance. Our counters were covered in huge trays of bread, buns and focaccia, not to mention cakes, cookies and pies, all while we were trying to serve our ever-crazier lunch and dinner rushes.

After a while we enlisted Silverstein's for our bread needs and, luckily, found New Moon Kitchen to provide our desserts and cornbread. New Moon is a small bakery run by childhood best friends Eden Hertzog and Shoshana Gehring. Lifelong vegetarians, Eden and Shoshana had always found that delicious, healthy vegan desserts were hard to come by. To fill that void in the marketplace, they began experimenting with vegan dessert recipes at home before venturing into the world of professional baking. In the beginning they worked from a small restaurant called Imagine Café, doing all the baking themselves, with Eden's dad making deliveries. With regular orders coming in from Juice for Life, though, New Moon's production went into overdrive. Eden and Shoshana baked through the night to provide fresh muffins, cookies and cakes by morning. The girls' philosophy, to provide handmade baked goods without preservatives, refined flours or refined sugars, or any animal products or by-products, has served them well. Today, they supply more than 40 stores and restaurants.

As New Moon grew, so did we. When our third location opened, we felt it was time to bring in some new vegan desserts to add to the New Moon selection. We were lucky to find Ilana Kadonoff of Sweets from the Earth Bakery. An occupational therapist by training, Ilana had always had a passion for baking and eventually left her practice in Toronto to train and work as a pastry chef in B.C. Returning to Toronto, she soon struck out on her own. Ilana, a vegetarian, decided to focus on vegan baking to cater to those clients whose dietary restrictions had previously precluded sweet indulgences (some of her clients' children, for instance, had egg and nut allergies, and had never before eaten a birthday cake). Her baked creations are a testament to the fact that you don't have to use cream, butter or eggs to make decadent, mouth-watering cakes or cookies.

Eden, Shoshana and Ilana have been gracious enough to share a few of their recipes with us. We hope you enjoy them as much as we do.

# orange cake with chocolate ganache

This New Moon Kitchen recipe makes a delightfully decadent Bundt cake, but it can also be baked as 6 jumbo or 12 regular muffins.

3 cups organic light spelt flour

1 cup raw, unrefined sugar

1 tsp sea salt

1-1/2 tsp baking soda

1/2 tsp baking powder
   (preferably non-aluminum)

1 cup orange zest (from approximately
   2 large oranges)

2 large oranges, juiced

1 cup vanilla soymilk

1/3 cup sunflower oil

1 tbsp pure vanilla extract

1/3 cup semi-sweet dairy-free chocolate
   chips (optional)

1 batch Chocolate Ganache (page 157)

1.  Oil a 10-inch Bundt pan.
2.  Mix flour, sugar, salt, baking soda, baking powder and orange zest in a medium-sized bowl. Set aside.
3.  Combine orange juice, soymilk, oil and vanilla in a separate bowl.
4.  Add wet ingredients to dry ingredients and mix thoroughly. Add chocolate chips (if using).
5.  Pour batter into the Bundt pan.
6.  Bake at 350°F for approximately 45 minutes or until a toothpick inserted into the centre comes out clean. (For muffins, sprinkle a little raw, unrefined sugar over the batter in each cup before baking for a yummy crunchy topping. Bake for only 30 minutes or until the tops are slightly browned.) Set aside to cool.
7.  When cooled, remove from pan and place on serving platter.
8.  Drizzle Chocolate Ganache over cake.
9.  Cool for 5 minutes and serve.

# chocolate ganache

A ganache is traditionally made with cream, but this vegan version is just as delectable. Use it as a topping for the Orange Cake (page 156), or as a sauce on your favourite dessert. Use a double boiler (a pot of simmering water with a stainless steel bowl resting on top) to melt the chocolate chips for this recipe. Be careful not to get any water droplets in your chocolate as it's melting or it will seize up and form lumps. If this does happen, just add a couple of drops of sunflower oil and keep stirring; it should loosen up and become smooth again.

**1 cup semi-sweet dairy-free chocolate chips**
**1/3 cup vanilla soymilk**

1. Melt chocolate chips in a double boiler.
2. Stir in soymilk as soon as chocolate chips have melted. Remove from heat immediately when mixture is fully combined and smooth.
3. Pour over dessert.

MAKES ENOUGH TO COVER 1 CAKE

# sweet potato pie

This recipe, an excellent alternative to pumpkin pie, is one of our favourite New Moon Kitchen recipes.

You will need some special equipment for this crust recipe, including a hand blender, rolling pin, food processor and a 10-1/2-inch deep-dish pie plate. In place of the traditional shortening or butter, New Moon has developed an oil emulsion that is a much healthier alternative.

**CRUST**

3 cups organic light spelt flour

1/4 cup raw, unrefined sugar

1/4 tsp baking soda

1 tsp cinnamon

3/4 tsp sea salt

2/3 cup sunflower oil

2 tsp liquid soy lecithin

1/3 cup boiling water

**SWEET POTATO FILLING**

4 large sweet potatoes, peeled and diced

3/4 cup soft silken tofu

2 tbsp grated fresh ginger, any juices reserved

1 tsp sea salt

1-1/2 tsp cinnamon

3/4 tsp nutmeg

1 cup maple syrup or brown sugar

1/3 cup sunflower oil

CRUST

1. Oil and flour a pie plate.
2. In a medium-sized bowl, combine flour, sugar, baking soda, cinnamon and salt. Set aside.
3. To make oil emulsion, combine sunflower oil, liquid soy lecithin and boiling water in a tall measuring cup or pitcher. Blend immediately with a hand blender until the mixture has a light, mayonnaise-like texture.
4. Add oil emulsion to dry ingredients and mix thoroughly.
5. Roll dough on a floured surface into a 14-inch round and lay into the greased pie plate.
6. Trim and flute or pinch the edges. Pierce the bottom and sides with fork.
7. Bake for 15 minutes at 350°F and cool.

### SWEET POTATO FILLING

1. Bring a pot of water to a boil and add sweet potatoes. Cook 10 to 15 minutes until tender; remove from heat and drain. Set aside.
2. In food processor, blend silken tofu until totally smooth.
3. Squeeze grated ginger in your hand or in a cheesecloth and reserve the juice. Discard pulp.
4. Add cooked sweet potatoes, ginger juice, salt, cinnamon, nutmeg, maple syrup and oil to tofu in food processor. Blend thoroughly.
5. Pour filling into cooled pie crust and bake at 350°F for 25 to 30 minutes, or until top is slightly browned. Remove from oven and cool before serving.

# lemon poppy seed bread

This wonderful New Moon recipe can be baked as one large loaf, or as four mini loaves.

4 cups organic light spelt flour

1-1/3 cups (approx.) raw, unrefined sugar

2 tsp baking soda

1 tsp baking powder

1 tsp sea salt

3/4 cup poppy seeds

Zest of 2 lemons

3 lemons, juiced

1/2 cup vanilla soymilk

1/2 cup sunflower oil

1 tsp pure vanilla extract

1 cup filtered water

1.  Oil and flour a 9- × 5-inch loaf pan. Set aside.
2.  In a large mixing bowl, stir together spelt flour, sugar, baking soda, baking powder, salt, poppy seeds and lemon zest. Set aside.
3.  In a small bowl, combine lemon juice with vanilla soymilk. Add to dry ingredients in mixing bowl but do not stir yet.
4.  Add sunflower oil, vanilla and water to dry ingredients. Mix wet and dry ingredients thoroughly.
5.  Pour batter into loaf pan and sprinkle top with raw, unrefined sugar.
6.  Bake for approximately 1 hour at 350°F or until a toothpick inserted in the centre comes out clean. (Bake approximately 45 minutes for mini loaves.)

# chocolate almond peanut butter pie

This is a Sweets from the Earth original. Any combination of nut butter and toasted nuts can be substituted.

**CRUST**
1-1/2 cups vegan chocolate
cookie crumbs
1 tbsp canola oil
1/4 cup maple syrup

**FILLING**
3/4 cup natural smooth
peanut butter
1/4 cup raw, unrefined sugar
1/4 cup maple syrup
1/2 cup + 1 tbsp firm silken tofu
1/4 cup + 2 tbsp vanilla soymilk
Pinch sea salt

**TOPPING**
1/2 cup vanilla soymilk
4 oz bittersweet chocolate,
chopped
1/4 cup + 2 tbsp almonds,
toasted and chopped

### CRUST

1. In a mixing bowl, combine cookie crumbs, oil and maple syrup. Press into an oiled 9-inch Pyrex pie plate.
2. Bake at 350°F for 10 minutes, remove from oven and set aside. Reduce oven temperature to 300°F.

### FILLING

1. In a food processor, blend together peanut butter, sugar, maple syrup, tofu, soymilk and salt until smooth. Pour into crust and bake for 15 minutes. Cool.

### TOPPING

1. In a small saucepan, bring soymilk to a boil. Remove from heat, add chocolate and stir until smooth.
2. Pour chocolate mixture over pie and sprinkle nuts on top.
3. Refrigerate at least 2 hours and serve.

# strawberry lavender muffins

These Sweets from the Earth muffins are absolutely divine. Feel free to use any kind of berry you fancy.

1-1/4 cups vanilla soymilk

3/4 cup + 1 tbsp maple syrup

1-1/2 tbsp dried lavender

1 cup applesauce (unsweetened)

4 cups organic light spelt flour

1/2 cup raw, unrefined sugar

1 tbsp baking powder

1 tsp baking soda

1/2 cup diced fresh strawberries

1/4 cup + 2 tbsp canola oil

1. Oil the muffin pans or use paper muffin pan liners.
2. Heat soymilk, maple syrup and lavender in a saucepan, and bring to a boil over medium heat.
3. Remove from heat, cover and infuse for 5 minutes. Strain mixture through a fine sieve and add applesauce. Set aside and cool completely.
4. Combine flour, sugar, baking power and baking soda in a large mixing bowl.
5. Add strawberries and toss to coat.
6. Add liquid and oil to dry ingredients. Mix gently just until mixture comes together. Do not overmix.
7. Scoop into muffin pans.
8. Bake at 350°F approximately 25 minutes or until tops spring back when lightly pressed.
9. Remove from muffin pans, cool and serve.

MAKES 12 MUFFINS

# fresh
## juice recipes

# the fresh juice bar

What makes a great juice bar?

A great juice bar will seduce you and draw you back again and again, tantalizing your juice buds with unique and delicious combinations. It is a natural oasis in an urban desert of frozen concentrates and pasteurized juices. It can also be a powerful catalyst that propels you to create your very own oasis of health and well-being at home. A positive juice experience has the power to awaken a person to the joys of juicing and a proactive approach to vibrant good health. When asked, people can often trace their love affair with juicing back to their very first taste of a freshly squeezed fruit or vegetable juice. One day, we hope every neighbourhood will have a truly awesome juice bar to get the juices flowing and imaginations going.

Doctors and nutritionists recommend at least five servings a day of fruits and vegetables. However, this can be difficult to manage if you are a typically busy person in today's world. Although the fibre content of fresh fruits and vegetables definitely has an important place in our diets, drinking our nutrition is an easier and quicker way to get maximum results. Solid food takes much longer for the body to digest in the stomach before its nourishment is finally ready to be distributed to the body's cells, tissues and organs. Removing the fibres enables nutrient-rich juices to be digested and absorbed more efficiently with a minimal amount of energy and effort.

Freshly squeezed juice drenches your body with revitalizing nutrients and leaves you feeling energized and balanced. Raw fruit and vegetable juices are a rich, concentrated source of vitamins, minerals, trace elements, protein, essential fatty acids, complex carbohydrates, phytochemicals and live enzymes.

Fresh fruit and vegetable juice, herbal tinctures and supplements can cleanse and detoxify you, boost your immune system, soothe your nerves, stimulate your brain and energize your body. Tailoring the individual properties and benefits of each ingredient to suit your needs is where the fun in juicing begins. Our approach at Fresh is to choose ingredients for their healthful benefits as well as for their texture, colour and flavour.

Making great tasting fresh juice cocktails, smoothies and shakes at home is really easy. All you need is a good juicer, a blender and a nearby grocery store that stocks high-quality produce. You'll soon discover that making your favourite combinations at home is easy, fast and economical. Before you know it, you'll be thinking of opening up your own juice bar!

Once you start juicing, don't get into a rut by making the same combinations over and over. Visit juice bars to discover new ways of using ingredients in interesting combinations. Unusual ingredients that we've recently discovered at Juice Lab, a wonderful juice bar in Nosara, Costa Rica, are avocado, granola, whole espresso beans, coconut water, bee pollen and liquid chlorophyll.

You will need a blender, juicer or both to prepare these recipes. Wherever possible we have given you amounts for store-bought juice in case you don't have a juicer at home.

# juicy tips

Juicing is an acquired skill that is fun, creative and easy to learn. A working knowledge of basic juicing guidelines, the right equipment, high-quality ingredients and fresh produce are all you require. This chapter is full of tips and techniques from our juice bars to help you make great juice.

## JUICERS

A juicer can unlock the goodness in fresh fruits and vegetables and deliver it quickly and easily to you. However, just how much of that goodness ends up in your glass depends on your juicer. A high-quality, efficient juicer will extract a smooth enzyme-rich juice and expel a moisture-free pulp. The drier the pulp, the more juice in the glass.

Today, there are a growing number of good-looking quality home juicers on the market to choose from, ranging in price from $125 (basic) to $350 (deluxe). These are sold at most upscale health food stores and department stores. Although it is true that you get what you pay for when purchasing a home juicer, our experience has proven that it is wise to earn your juicing stripes with an inexpensive juicer first before you go for the ultra deluxe model. Once you are hooked and juicing regularly you will probably want to upgrade your home juicer. Keep in mind that an attractive juicer on the kitchen counter is likely to be used more often than one hidden away in the cupboard where it is out of sight and out of mind.

Citrus attachments are often sold separately from juicers. These attachments are unnecessary, however, if you have a centrifugal juicer. A centrifugal juicer will juice most fruits and vegetables, with the exception of wheat grass. At Fresh, we peel all citrus fruit and run them through the centrifugal juicers. This method produces a creamier, smoother juice and also tends to be faster and less messy than using the citrus attachment. In our opinion, the true measure of a home juicer is how well it juices fine leafy greens, achieving a high yield of juice and a fine pulp.

If you are shopping around for a good home juicer, look for these essential features, which are the same as in our own industrial juicers:

- centrifugal (spinning) force
- automatic pulp ejection
- a quiet and powerful motor (1/3 to 3/4 hp)
- stainless steel bowl, blade and basket
- large feeder or hopper tube
- removable parts that are easy to clean and quick to reassemble
- rubber feet
- two- to five-year warranty

Home juicers with these recommended qualities include Omega 4000, L'Equip221, Juiceman II and the Juicelady JL500.

## THE SCIENCE OF JUICING

Firm fruits and vegetables with a high water content, such as apples, pears, carrots, broccoli, parsnips, celery and cucumber, should be juiced, not blended. A juicer will easily separate the water from the fibre in these foods. At Fresh we prefer to juice our pineapples and all melons, although they are also delicious puréed in the blender.

Leafy greens—such as parsley, cilantro, beet greens, chard, cabbage, kale or spinach—should only be juiced. The nutrients within these foods are contained in the juice, which must be separated from the fibre for maximum results. A centrifugal juicer will spin the greens, extracting the juice while expelling the fibre. Juiced greens are an important factor in nutrient-rich and enzyme-packed combinations. Always juice a higher-water content ingredient after a leafy green vegetable to flush the concentrated juice from the juicer.

As a general rule, start the juicing sequence with the ingredients that have the highest concentration of flavour and end with more neutral ingredients. This method will ensure that strong, pungent flavours (ginger, garlic, beets, peppers, parsley and spinach for instance) will be flushed out by the more neutral ingredients, guaranteeing that your next juice will not be tainted.

Juicing a neutral ingredient last also allows you to adjust the flavour and potency of the drink. Neutral juices such as carrot or cucumber enhance and balance the powerful effects of other, more pungent juices, such as garlic, ginger, beet and spinach, which should initially be used in small doses.

We have three basic vegetable juices—carrot, celery and cucumber—that combine with other stronger-flavoured juices to create good-tasting healthful vegetable cocktails.

Experiment with your own combinations. Using the above juicing guidelines, choose one of your favourite basic juice ingredients along with two stronger-flavoured ingredients. If you like the concoction you have just created, build on it by adding more ingredients using the same ratio to create a new combo.

## BASIC JUICES

Carrot, celery, cucumber

## STRONG JUICES

Ginger, garlic, parsley, cilantro, kale, spinach, beet, beet greens, Swiss chard, parsnip, broccoli, cabbage, red or green pepper, lemon, lime

## ACCENTS

Cayenne pepper, hot sauce, crushed chili peppers, nutmeg

## JUICE PREP

We recommend that you use organically grown produce whenever possible to avoid pesticide and herbicide residue and to make the purest juices possible. If you cannot access organic produce, we suggest you peel your fruits and vegetables first.

Before juicing, wash all produce and remove any bruised or mouldy areas. Peel all citrus, melons and pineapples; these peels are bitter and are very hard on the juicer motor and blades. The skins of most other fruits and vegetables, including garlic and ginger, may be left on. Remove pits from peaches or plums before juicing as they can damage the delicate blade and screen of the machine. Seeds from lemons, limes, apples, pears and all melons need not be removed because the juicer will spit them out.

Cut fruits and vegetables to fit the size of your juicer's hopper (the hole that feeds the juicer).

Although vegetable and fruit juice will not spoil if refrigerated, the flavour, colour and potency will decline quickly. It's always best to drink freshly squeezed juice right after you make it.

Be sure to thoroughly clean your home juicer immediately after you use it to avoid clogging the screen with hard, dried bits of pulp.

## BLENDERS

We use digital high-powered blenders at all three of our Fresh locations. All of our blenders have Plexiglas sound enclosures to reduce the noise level. The digital settings allow us to preset the blending times and speeds so we can go on to other things while the juices are blending. Most blenders are available in commercial-use and home-use models. We prefer to use Plexiglas blender jugs because they are lighter in weight and tend to last longer than glass. A stainless steel jug, while easy to clean, obstructs the view of the juice blending, which is not practical in a busy juice bar setting. In the beginning, before we reached the kind of volume that we have now at our juice bars, we worked with Hamilton Beach blenders. Today, we work with Vita-Mix commercial blenders.

Look for these characteristics when buying a new blender:

- a 32–48 oz Plexiglas blender jug
- high, low and pulse switch
- a quiet and powerful motor
- a thick, strong lid with removable hopper
- removable parts that are easy to clean and quick to reassemble

## THE ART OF BLENDING

Fleshy fruits and vegetables such as bananas, avocados, berries, tomatoes, kiwi, peaches and mango, are better blended rather than juiced. Separating the water from the fibre of soft fruits and vegetables is very difficult for juice extractors. The fleshy fibre tends to clog up the screen inside the juicer, and a great deal of precious juice is expelled with the pulp.

Blending is the best way to get the most out of these, often expensive, ingredients.

When blending milk shakes and fruit smoothies, be sure you have enough of a base liquid to liquefy your other ingredients. Use no more than 1 cup of ice per serving as too much ice will create a thick slush and it is very hard on the blender. When blending juice, always start on the lowest setting and then switch to a higher setting once the ingredients have been puréed. This will extend the life of your blade and motor. Keep the lid on and use the removable hopper to add ingredients midway if necessary. Add powdered supplements last to prevent them from sticking to the sides of the blender.

A blended fruit smoothie or shake at Fresh always starts with a basic fruit juice or dairy-free milk, which acts as the liquefying ingredient. The amount of liquid used in proportion to the amount of whole ingredients will determine the thickness and texture of the drink. We make our smoothies with freshly squeezed juice, whole fruit and ice. There are no hidden ingredients in our drinks—what you see is exactly what you get. We also add hulled hemp seeds, sunflower sprouts, dates, coconut milk, nut butters, spices, maple syrup or honey for additional flavour and depth.

There are seven basic fruit juices on our menu—orange, grapefruit, pineapple, watermelon, apple, pear and mango. Buying natural or organic bottled papaya, passion fruit, lichee or grape juice opens up an even wider range of possibilities for creating new blended smoothies at home. Check the labels to avoid sugars, concentrates and preservatives.

Sweet, creamy, dairy-free milks make an ideal substitute for cow or goat's milk. Organic vanilla soymilk and rice milk are used as the liquid base for our selection of shakes. Other yummy and nutritious dairy-free alternatives include almond milk and oat milk.

At Fresh, we boost our fruit smoothies and shakes with a variety of supplements, protein powders, herbal tinctures, wheat grass, fresh yogurt, coconut, nut butters, dried fruit, spices and natural sweeteners to create our special menu of vital fluids, energy elixirs, lassis, power shakes and super power shakes. Our juice cocktails, smoothies and shakes provide a delicious liquid backdrop that enhances the benefits of added nutritional boosts. Blending supplements and herbal tinctures with liquids also ensures their easy and quick absorption.

Choose from the following list to create your own new combinations, using the above-mentioned blending guidelines.

## BASIC FRUIT JUICES

Orange, grapefruit, pineapple, watermelon, apple, pear, mango

## MILKS

Soymilk, rice milk, almond milk, oat milk

## WHOLE FRUITS

Banana, strawberry, blueberry, kiwi, raspberry

## ACCENTS

Hulled hemp seeds, fresh yogurt, dates, sunflower sprouts, almond butter, peanut butter, tahini, coconut milk, brewed espresso, whole espresso beans, chai concentrate, avocado, cinnamon, cloves, nutmeg, lemon, ginger, quick-cooking oats

## SWEETENERS

Honey; maple syrup; raw, unrefined sugar

## SUPPLEMENTS

Spirulina, Greens +, Nu-Life Propel, Ultra WheyMore Protein, GeniSoy Protein, wheat grass, echinacea, milk thistle, kava kava, gingko biloba, ginseng, royal jelly, vitamin C powder, bee pollen, chlorophyll

# wheat grass

In the juicing world, wheat grass is considered the caviar of all juices. Like caviar, wheat grass has a devoted following, is an acquired taste and is consumed by the ounce. It is the most costly of all juices. Wheat grass has an almost mystical aura of goodness surrounding it and is one of those foods that we know is really good for us. We'll try to explain why.

Through photosynthesis plants convert the sun's energy to produce chlorophyll and then release oxygen into the atmosphere. All plants contain chlorophyll; however, the greener the plant the more chlorophyll it contains. When we eat or drink our greens, we are taking in the sun's energy, which gives life to all living things.

The molecular structure of chlorophyll is almost identical to that of red blood cells, the oxygen-carrying hemoglobin. It's no wonder then that chlorophyll is often referred to as "the blood of plant life." Raw chlorophyll oxygenates, purifies, regenerates and enriches the blood and the body's organs. It fights bacterial growth, promotes healthy intestinal flora and detoxifies the liver, kidneys and blood.

Dr. Ann Wigmore, a pioneering health educator, was the first to popularize the powerful healing properties of wheat grass, sprouts and a living-foods diet when she founded the world-renowned Hippocrates Health Institute in Boston, in 1963. Wheat grass, a member of the cereal grass group, is a nutrient-rich sprout with a high chlorophyll content. According to Dr. Wigmore, one pound of fresh wheat grass is equal in nutritional value to nearly 25 pounds of vegetables because wheat grass, abundant in protein, can absorb up to 90 of the estimated 102 minerals found in fertile soil. For this reason it should always be grown organically. Wheat grass also has a higher concentration of helpful digestive enzymes and antioxidants than most other foods. People allergic to wheat or other cereal grains are almost never allergic to them in their grass stage.

Wheat grass can be grown indoors or outdoors. Indoors, organic wheat berries are sprouted in trays and grown for approximately five days until harvest. A specific wheat grass juicer or press is needed to extract the juice from the fine blades of grass. Unlike a regular juicer, which shreds the fibres, a grass juicer presses and squeezes the pulp—like wringing out a wet towel. We use a motorized Wheateena wheat grass juicer; Teldon is another excellent motorized wheat grass juicer. A manual version of the Wheateena juicer is available at less cost.

Drink wheat grass immediately after juicing. A rapid deterioration of the sensitive enzymes and nutrients occurs when the juice is separated from the fibre that protects it. All enzymes and nutrients in fresh juice deteriorate quickly once separated from pulp. However, the deterioration of wheat grass is especially fast; the best way to store it is by flash freezing. Purchase flash-frozen wheat grass at your health food store and store in the freezer until you are ready to drink it. It is preferable to drink wheat grass on an empty stomach to get the maximum benefits from this potent juice. However, if you are a first-timer or are still getting used to the taste and effects of it, mix it into a smoothie, which will offset the immediate effects of the wheat grass and allow it to metabolize more gradually in your system.

Occasionally, mild nausea is experienced after drinking wheat grass, which can be a consequence of the immediate and powerful release of toxins taking place in the body. The end result is an energy boost, a stimulating mental and physical high that lasts all day. The effects are similar to caffeine or sugar but without the crash at the end.

Fresh-pressed wheat grass tastes sweet, with a hint of licorice. It is like sucking on a thousand blades of young green grass all at once. It is an acquired taste for some, while others adore it instantly. One to two ounces a day helps to maintain a healthy immune system and body.

# energy elixirs

Our elixirs are combinations of ingredients that, when taken together, are thought to boost an individual's energy levels. It can be as seemingly simple as a Raspberry Lemonade (very hydrating and high in vitamin C), or as intense as a Brazilian Immune Boost, a fortifying and cleansing combination of beet, ginger, orange, lemon, echinacea and goldenseal.

Every elixir we make contains a nutritional supplement or main ingredient such as ginseng, echinacea, spirulina, whey protein, hulled hemp seeds, sunflower sprouts, oats or tahini. These are featured against a delicious liquid backdrop of soymilk or freshly squeezed juice.

Every ingredient—whether beet, parsnip, ginger, pear, raspberry, banana, orange, apple or strawberry—is chosen not only for the concentrated nutrients it possesses but also for its ability to seduce us with flavour and colour. Explore the range of elixirs offered in this section and, soon enough, you'll be creating your own combinations.

# ginseng sunset

At Fresh we have an ongoing love affair with the pear. To the Chinese, it represents longevity, justice and good judgment. To others, the pear is a traditional symbol of good health, fortune and hope. Pears make beautiful juice and combine with strawberries and oranges to produce a fruity cocktail that is extremely high in vitamin C and rejuvenating, subtle and sweet. Chinese panax ginseng, considered the most stimulating of all the ginsengs, is extremely helpful in relieving stress and fatigue. The ginseng root extract, cultivated for centuries in China and revered by its people, is also reputed to improve mental and physical performance, stamina, endurance and resistance to infection.

We prefer a firm, medium-ripe pear for efficient juicing. Overly ripe pears clog juicer baskets, so just add a little filtered water to flush the juice through the machine.

**3 pears**
**4 oranges, peeled**
**3 tbsp strawberries, fresh or frozen**
**3 cubes ice**
**1 vial panax ginseng**

1. Juice the pears and oranges first. Blend with strawberries and ice until smooth.
2. Pour into a glass. Swirl in the vial of ginseng and serve.

SERVES 1–2

# brazilian immune boost

Customers returning from their travels often share tales and takeout menus of juice bars from around the world. That's how we learned of the unlikely combination of freshly squeezed beet and orange juice being served in juice bars throughout Brazil. Skeptical yet curious, we discovered that beets and citrus do in fact work very well together. If you're feeling under the weather this fortifying and cleansing juice is a good choice.

Rich in antioxidant vitamins A, B complex and C, folic acid and minerals, beets are a highly nutritious tonic to the immune system. They add body and an earthy sweetness to this drink.

Ginger root relieves nausea and indigestion while also helping to warm the body by improving circulation.

Lemon and orange, both high in vitamin C, help boost the immune system. Try substituting pink grapefruit for orange to reduce the sweetness and increase the cleansing effects. Or, for an extra boost, add a dash of cayenne pepper, one of the highest sources of botanic vitamin C.

Echinacea is possibly the most widely used herb for boosting the immune system against colds and flu in the beginning stages. Another little known fact is echinacea's ability to rid the body of dead cells and other waste products by stimulating lymphatic drainage.

Goldenseal is effective in fighting a cold or the flu once the infection has taken hold, by reducing inflammation and stimulating the immune system's response.

**2 beets, small**
**1/2 inch fresh ginger**
**1/2 lemon, peeled**
**6 oranges, peeled**
**20 drops echinacea tincture**
**20 drops goldenseal tincture**

1. Juice the beet, ginger, lemon and oranges.
2. Pour into a glass. Drop in the echinacea and goldenseal tinctures; serve.

SERVES 1–2

# out of my head WARM

This elixir is designed to soothe the head, relax the mind and please the taste buds, of course. Parsnips add a sweet creamy spiced flavour to this combination, which is greatly enhanced when gently heated. Parsnips are a good source of potassium, silica, vitamin C and sulphur.

In both the Ayurvedic tradition of India and traditional Chinese medicine, ginger is known for its ability not only to warm and invigorate the body but also to enhance clarity of mind and relieve headaches.

Apples stimulate the appetite and promote good digestion due to the presence of malic and tartaric acids, which inhibit growth of bacteria in the digestive tract. The pectin in apples draws cholesterol and toxins out of the body. Apples are also cleansing to the liver and gallbladder. Red eating apples, such as Gala or McIntosh, are the best for juicing.

Feverfew is known to provide relief from headaches and migraines.

This combination is also delicious served cold.

**1/2 inch fresh ginger**
**3 parsnips**
**6 apples**
**20 drops feverfew tincture**
**1 shake cinnamon**

1. Juice the ginger, parsnips and apples.
2. Steam or warm in a saucepan without letting the liquid come to a boil. Drop in the feverfew tincture and pour into a mug.
3. Garnish with cinnamon and serve.

SERVES 1–2

# relax to the max WARM

This drink is a great comfort when there's no end in sight to the cold grey days of winter. Oats make an excellent nerve tonic for anyone suffering from anxiety or nervous exhaustion. Rich in protein, minerals and vitamin A, oats are also a great energy food for physically active people. Oat drinks have been consumed in Europe for centuries to strengthen the sick and elderly.

Dates are a rich source of magnesium and potassium. (A magnesium deficiency interferes with the transmission of nerve and muscle impulses, causing irritability and nervousness.) Honey dates are the best for shakes.

Maple syrup, a delicious natural sweetener, is the boiled-down sap of the sugar maple tree. It takes 40 gallons of sap to produce 1 gallon of syrup. Maple syrup contains approximately 35 percent less sucrose than processed white sugar. (Refined sugar is acid forming and highly addictive, and leads to an imbalance of blood sugar levels.) Grade C is the least processed of the maple syrups and ranks highest in mineral content. It is available in bulk at most natural food stores.

Cinnamon improves resistance to the stresses of everyday life by warming the body and invigorating the nervous system. Cinnamon also possesses powerful antibacterial, antiviral and antifungal properties that are useful in fighting infection.

The gentle sedative effects of passion flower help relieve anxiety, hyperactivity and insomnia.

**2 tbsp quick-cooking oats**

**6 dates, pitted**

**8 oz filtered water, hot**

**1 tsp maple syrup**

**20 drops passion flower tincture**

**1 shake cinnamon**

1. Combine the oats, dates and hot water. Let soak for 5 minutes. Blend with maple syrup until smooth.
2. Pour in a mug and drop in the passion flower tincture.
3. Garnish with cinnamon and serve.

SERVES 1–2

# stomach soother

Carrots were used by the ancient Greeks as a tonic for the stomach and as a remedy for flatulence. Carrots were first cultivated in Afghanistan and the ancient Near East hundreds of years ago. The carrot is a storehouse of nutrients—vitamins A, B and C; iron; calcium; and potassium—and they are one of the richest sources of beta carotene (the antioxidant that protects against cancer). Carrots are alkaline forming and very helpful in relieving stomach acid and heartburn by reducing irritation and inflammation. Carrot juice is known to be very helpful in increasing the milk supply of nursing moms. Carrots make a good base for adding other juices; if you find carrot juice too sweet alone, cut it with a vegetable such as cucumber or celery to reduce the sweetness.

Chamomile is a calming herb useful in treating anxiety, insomnia, flatulence and gastritis. Fennel is renowned for its soothing effect on the digestive system, and catnip eases stomach and intestinal cramps.

**6 carrots**
**15 drops chamomile tincture**
**15 drops fennel tincture**
**15 drops catnip tincture**

1. Juice the carrots. Pour into a glass.
2. Drop in the tinctures of chamomile, fennel and catnip. Serve.

SERVES 1–2

# kidney cocktail

This delicious vegetable cocktail is sweet, light and nourishing. Spinach is considered a blood builder due to its rich iron and chlorophyll content. Nicknamed the "smooth mover," spinach has a mild laxative effect.

Apples are a rich source of vitamins, minerals and trace elements. They aid digestion, help regulate acidity in the stomach, and have a cleansing and detoxifying effect on the liver and kidneys.

Cucumber, a natural diuretic that is 96 percent water, counteracts toxins and purifies the skin. It has a cooling effect on the system and aids in preventing fluid retention. Cucumber skin is also high in silicon and chlorophyll, which benefit the skin, hair and nails.

Dandelion improves kidney, spleen and pancreas function. It acts as a diuretic and cleanses the blood and liver. Young dandelion leaves can be juiced or eaten in salads. Uva ursi, a medicinal herb, promotes excretion of fluids and fights bacteria. It is useful for bladder and kidney infections and prostate disorders.

**4 medium carrots**
**1 handful spinach**
**2 apples**
**1/2 cucumber**
**1/2 lemon, peeled**
**20 drops dandelion tincture**
**20 drops uva ursi tincture**

1. Juice the carrots, spinach, apples, cucumber and lemon.
2. Pour into a glass. Drop in the dandelion and uva ursi tinctures; serve.

SERVES 1–2

# in the raw

Apple juice and sunflower sprouts may sound like an unlikely combination for a blended drink, but the result is truly wonderful, extremely energizing and rejuvenating. These two ingredients are a good foundation for many more ingredients.

Sweet and tasty sunflower seeds are at the peak of their nutritional and enzymatic vitality when sprouted. Although many delicious sprouts are good for eating, the sunflower sprout is the best for blending into juices.

Hulled hemp seeds have a delicious nutty flavour. They are second only to the soybean as a source of complete vegetable protein. Hemp seeds contain all eight essential amino acids that humans need, in the right proportions. They also contain a generous amount of omega 3 and omega 6, essential fatty acids.

Hulled hemp seeds are good for making smoothies. Unhulled hemp seeds make the drink gritty and the shells often get caught between your teeth.

**6 apples**
**1 cup sunflower sprouts**
**1 banana, peeled**
**1 tbsp hulled hemp seeds (page 19)**
**3 cubes ice**

1. Juice the apples.
2. Blend the apple juice with sunflower sprouts, banana, hulled hemp seeds and ice until smooth.
3. Pour into a glass and serve.

SERVES 1–2

# blueberry thrills

This creamy blend is a beautiful deep blue-purple due partly to the blue pigment phycocyanin in spirulina, rarely found in other foods in such generous amounts. Phycocyanin is said to stimulate the brain and increase mental capacity.

Spirulina, a microalgae, is harvested in hot sunny climates around the world. It is sometimes likened to "manna from heaven" because it contains the full spectrum of nutrients in concentrations unlike any other single grain, herb or plant on earth. Spirulina contains high doses of ten essential nutrients: vitamins A, B1, B2 and B12; niacin; calcium; phosphorous; magnesium; iron and protein. The protein digestibility of spirulina is rated at 85 percent, versus about 20 percent for beef. These nutrients are most beneficial for stress-related mental and physical fatigue, iron deficiency, and kidney and liver detoxification, and for boosting the immune system. We use Hawaiian Organic Spirulina by Nu-Life. Spirulina tastes like the ocean, mildly salty and fishy; however, the flavour won't be dominant when it's added to a juice or shake.

Let's not forget the blueberries, which are high in vitamin C and antioxidants and also taste great. All berries should be blended, rather than juiced, to reduce wastage.

**1 tsp spirulina**
**3 tbsp blueberries, fresh or frozen**
**1 banana, peeled**
**1 cup vanilla soymilk**
**3 cubes ice**

1. Blend spirulina, blueberries, banana, soymilk and ice until smooth.
2. Pour into a glass and serve.

SERVES 1–2

# superbuff

This combination was created in response to the growing number of requests from serious gym buffs looking for a high-protein shake before or after their workout. This was the first combination on our juice menu to include a whey-based protein powder. Whey, a normal by-product of cheese making, is the liquid left when the solids in milk come together and are pressed into solid form. Whey protein is produced by filtering and purifying whey liquid and then removing the water to produce a high-quality protein powder that is free of fat and milk sugar (lactose). Whey increases the body's production of muscle protein and helps to build lean body mass. This explains why it's popular among athletes and bodybuilders. It also helps to protect against muscle wasting in people with diseases such as AIDS. At your health food store, choose a whey protein that is preservative free and low in added fats and sugars. We recommend Ultra WheyMore Protein by Nu-Life.

For a breakfast version, try adding yogurt or honey or substituting another type of berry. Feel free to substitute the vanilla soymilk with rice milk or almond milk.

**3 tbsp raspberries, fresh or frozen**

**1 banana, peeled**

**1 cup vanilla soymilk**

**3 cubes ice**

**1 tbsp vanilla whey protein powder**

1. Blend raspberries, banana, soymilk, ice and whey protein powder until smooth.
2. Pour into a glass and serve.

SERVES 1–2

# beautylicious

This shake is a silky-smooth chocolate fix for active people. We use GeniSoy, a non-GMO soy protein that is fat free and gluten free. This combination is a fantastic base for new ingredients such as raspberries, espresso or peanut butter. For a thicker, creamier version, even higher in protein, use chocolate soymilk instead of rice milk.

Bananas are blended into our drinks to add volume, texture and sweetness. With their high natural sugar, potassium and magnesium content, bananas boost stamina. Overly ripe bananas can be stored in the freezer (peeled, in a freezer bag) for later use.

**1 banana, peeled**
**1 cup chocolate rice milk**
**1 tbsp chocolate soy protein powder**
**3 cubes ice**

1. Blend banana, chocolate rice milk, chocolate soy protein powder and ice until smooth.
2. Pour into a glass and serve.

SERVES 1–2

# chai chiller

In India, chai is a popular blend of aromatic spices such as ginger, cardamom, cinnamon, cloves, fennel and black tea sweetened generously with honey and hot milk. Traditional chai spices warm the body and greatly improve digestion. Chai is a nice tea to enjoy at the end of a big meal.

Stimulating to the system, much like coffee, chai may be brewed and stored in the fridge for blending morning shakes such as the Chai Chiller. Chai is available in health food stores as loose tea, tea bags or liquid concentrate. We like to use the liquid concentrate high-quality brand Sattwa Chai. Oregon Chai is also a good brand of liquid concentrate.

In the Chai Chiller, the traditional spiced chai is given a bit of a shakeup. Coconut milk, thick and sweet, fortifies and strengthens the whole body. In the Far East, it is commonly used to treat weakness, malnutrition and emaciation due to illness. Coconut milk is a thirst quencher and a good saturated fat, useful for vegetarians who need to keep their weight up. This shake is great to drink any time of the day.

**1/2 cup spiced chai concentrate**

**1/2 cup coconut milk**

**1 banana**

**1 cup vanilla soymilk**

**3 cubes ice**

1. Blend chai concentrate, coconut milk, banana, soymilk and ice until smooth.
2. Pour into a glass and serve.

SERVES 1–2

# promised land

This is a great dessert shake that tastes like halvah, the Middle Eastern delicacy. Tahini comprises hulled sesame seeds ground into butter. High in calories, it's a great ingredient for vegans who want to put on some weight. Add 1 tablespoon dark unsweetened cocoa for a truly decadent treat. This shake is also nice served warm.

**1 tbsp tahini**

**1 tsp honey**

**1 banana**

**1 cup vanilla soymilk**

**1 shake cinnamon**

**3 cubes ice**

1. Blend tahini, honey, banana, soymilk, cinnamon and ice until smooth.
2. Pour into a glass and serve.

SERVES 1–2

# banana oat milk WARM

The high starch content and nutritious qualities of bananas make a delicious breakfast shake. The combination of oats and banana has a calming effect. Originally from Eastern and Southern Europe, oat drinks and porridge were prescribed for insomnia, loss of appetite and constipation. At one time oats were eaten more than any other food in Italy; Leonardo da Vinci apparently loved to eat oats. Today, herbalists often use oat tea to help alleviate the symptoms of drug addicts suffering from withdrawal. The complex carbohydrate content of oats provides energizing fuel for the body, but they are also known to have a soothing effect on the nerves.

Cinnamon warms the body and enhances digestion, especially the metabolism of fats.

**2 tbsp quick-cooking oats**

**1 banana, peeled**

**1 cup filtered water, hot**

**1 tsp maple syrup**

**1 shake cinnamon**

1. Combine the oats, banana and hot water in a bowl. Soak for 5 minutes.
2. Blend with maple syrup until smooth.
3. Pour into a mug, garnish with cinnamon and serve.

SERVES 1–2

# maple lemonade

This recipe, including the cayenne pepper, also commonly known as the "master cleanser," is often used for fasting. This healthy lemonade is good for you and beneficial to drink anytime of the day. It is also a soothing cold remedy when gently heated and sprinkled with cayenne pepper. The high vitamin C content of the cayenne and lemon, combined with the rich mineral content of the maple syrup and the hydrating effects of drinking large amounts of filtered water are what make this lemonade more than just a pretty drink.

**2 lemons, peeled**
**1 cup filtered water**
**1 tbsp maple syrup, grade C**
**3 cubes ice**
**1 shake cayenne pepper (optional)**
**1/2 inch fresh ginger, sliced (optional)**

1. Juice or squeeze the lemons.
2. Blend with water, maple syrup, ice, cayenne and ginger (if using).
3. Pour into a glass or mug and serve.

SERVES 1–2

# raspberry lemonade

Raspberry lemonade is pink, pretty, thirst quenching and naturally high in vitamin C. Fresh mint leaves are a delicious accent to this drink.

**2 lemons, peeled**
**1 tbsp + 1 tsp raspberries, fresh or frozen**
**1-1/2 cups filtered water**
**1 tbsp raw, unrefined sugar**
**3 cubes ice**
**1 sprig fresh mint (optional)**

1. Juice or squeeze the lemons.
2. Blend with raspberries, water, sugar and ice.
3. Pour into a glass and garnish with mint (if using). Serve.

SERVES 1–2

# pro athletic shakes

The following three shakes were recently introduced on our juice menu. In this new group we included the kind of shakes we like to make for ourselves at the restaurant, before the doors open to the public. These shakes combine our favourite supplements with our most-loved ingredients. These are easy and fun to make at home.

# tour de force

Inspired by Lance Armstrong.

Go wild here! Substitute other kinds of berries such as strawberries, raspberries or blackberries and a spoonful of honey to keep this shake from getting too tart.

**3 tbsp blueberries**
**1 banana, peeled**
**3 tbsp yogurt**
**1 cup vanilla soymilk**
**1 tsp spirulina**
**1 tbsp vanilla whey protein powder**
**3 cubes ice**

1. Use a blender to combine blueberries, banana, yogurt, soymilk, spirulina, protein powder and ice until creamy and smooth.
2. Pour into a glass and serve.

SERVES 1–2

# swoosh

Peanut butter and bananas have a special affinity that is irresistible to most of us. Throw in chocolate and it's a match made in heaven.

But this really is a healthy shake to provide lots of energy. Greens + is a green superfood supplement that we like. Any green superfood supplement should have the grasses of barley, wheat and alfalfa as well as a selection of microalgae such as spirulina, chlorella, dulse and dunaliella. Beyond this, ingredients vary. Greens +, for instance, also has organically grown soy sprouts, antioxidant herbs and extracts, probiotic cultures and pectins, royal jelly and ginseng. With steady use, a good quality green superfood supplement will increase energy, improve stamina, sharpen mental alertness and cleanse toxins from the blood.

**1 tbsp natural peanut butter**

**1 banana, peeled**

**1 cup vanilla soymilk**

**1 tbsp maple syrup**

**1 tsp Greens +**

**1 tbsp chocolate whey protein powder**

**Pinch cinnamon**

**3 cubes ice**

1. Use a blender to combine peanut butter, banana, soymilk, maple syrup, Greens +, protein powder, cinnamon and ice until creamy and smooth.
2. Pour into a glass and serve.

SERVES 1–2

# cross-trainer

This mouth-watering shake is sweet, rich and smooth. The banana and mango provide plenty of complex carbohydrates while the soy protein and yogurt add calcium and protein.

**1 cup mango juice, bottled**

**3 tbsp fresh yogurt**

**1 banana, peeled**

**1 tsp honey**

**1 oz wheat grass, fresh or frozen**

**1 tbsp vanilla soy protein powder**

**3 cubes ice**

1. Use a blender to combine mango juice, yogurt, banana, honey, wheat grass, protein powder and ice until creamy and smooth.
2. Pour into a glass and serve.

SERVES 1–2

... Drog...
One Love          ...
Negril Beach      First Kiss
Rise & Shine      Breathless
                  Apple Pie HOT
Pink Flamingo

...WERSHAKES

## VEGETABLES

Sweet Surrender
Beet Root Frappé
OKC
Red Rocket
Detox Cocktail
Garden Cocktail
Flu Fighter

## REAL LEM...

Lemonade  16 oz $3⁰⁰ / 32 oz $5⁵⁰
Raspberry Lemonade  16 oz $3⁵⁰ / 32 oz $6⁰⁵

## PRO ATHLETIC SHAKES

16 oz $7⁷⁵ / 32 oz $15⁵⁰

### Tour de Force
blueberry / organic yogourt / vanilla soymilk / banana / Spirulina
Vanilla Ultra Wheymore Protein (55g.)

### Swoosh
peanut butter / banana / vanilla soymilk / maple syrup / cinnamon
Greens + / Chocolate Wheymore Protein (55g.)

### Cross Trainer
mango / organic yogourt / banana / honey / Organic Wheatgrass
Nu-Life Propel

Beer
Lager or Dark Ale
Red or White Wine
   glass $5⁹⁵    half litre $13⁹⁵
San Pellegrino $3⁰⁰
   limonata / aranciata

## DES...

Ask about our daily selection of
vegan desserts.

LOVE YOUR MOTHER

# lassis

The lassi is a traditional Far Eastern beverage, popular in India, Sri Lanka, Nepal, Malaysia and Indonesia. It is prepared with live yogurt, honey and any number of exotic spices and fruits. It is especially pleasant to drink after a heavy, spicy meal or as a liquid breakfast on the run.

We introduced organic live yogurt to our menu of supplements and herbal tinctures a couple of years ago. By approaching yogurt as a nutritional supplement with positive health benefits, we were able to justify introducing it as the first and only dairy product to make it onto our juice menu.

One of nature's wonder foods, yogurt is one of the best ways to add calcium to your diet and is highly beneficial to the digestive system when eaten regularly. Made when sour fermented milk is curdled by bacteria to a custard-like consistency, live yogurt contains *Lactobacillus bulgaricus* and *l. acidophilus*. In the bowel it reestablishes friendly bacteria and eliminates the overgrowth of unfriendly bacteria produced by unhealthy diets or through the use of antibiotics. Lactic acid in yogurt aids in the synthesis of B vitamins and increases the absorption of nutrients such as calcium and iron. It also regulates bowel function and relieves gas. Often those with lactose intolerance can digest yogurt.

# mango lassi

Use very fresh ripe mangoes if available or natural unsweetened mango juice. If you like, add 1/2 teaspoon each ground cardamom and cinnamon to stimulate the flow of digestive juices and further enhance the sweet flavours.

**1 mango, peeled and chopped**
**OR**
**1 cup mango juice, bottled**

**1 banana, peeled**
**3 tbsp yogurt**

**1 tsp honey**
**3 cubes ice**

1. Use a blender to combine mango or mango juice, banana, yogurt, honey and ice until creamy and smooth.
2. Pour into a glass and serve.

SERVES 1

# hemp lassi

The hemp seeds lend a rich nutty flavour to this combination. The dates act as a natural sweetener and combine nicely with the banana and yogurt. Adding spirulina will increase the protein content and energizing effects of this lassi. This is a high-octane breakfast or mid-afternoon shake guaranteed to keep you going.

**2 apples**
**OR**
**1 cup apple juice, bottled**

**1 tbsp hulled hemp seeds**
**6 dates, pitted**
**1 banana, peeled**

**3 tbsp yogurt**
**3 cubes ice**

1. Juice the apples first (if using).
2. Use a blender to combine the apple juice, hemp seeds, dates, banana, yogurt and ice until creamy and smooth.
3. Pour into a glass and serve.

SERVES 1

# strawberry lassi

Strawberry combinations are always a favourite on our menu. Add raspberries and blackberries for a three-berry lassi packed with vitamin C and bioflavanoids. Add honey to sweeten as necessary.

3 oranges, peeled
OR
1 cup orange juice, bottled

3 tbsp strawberries,
fresh or frozen
1 banana, peeled

3 tbsp yogurt
3 cubes ice

1. Juice the oranges first (if using).
2. Use a blender to combine the orange juice, strawberries, banana, yogurt and ice until creamy and smooth.
3. Pour into a glass and serve.

SERVES 1

# pear lassi

This lassi is exotic yet simple. You will get a much stronger flavour if you don't peel the pears. To spice this lassi up, increase the amount of ginger and add cloves and cinnamon.

3 pears
OR
1 cup pear juice, bottled

1/2 inch fresh ginger
3 tbsp fresh yogurt
3 cubes ice

1. Juice the pears and ginger first. Blend with yogurt and ice until creamy and smooth.
2. Pour into a glass and serve.

SERVES 1

# glossary

**adobo sauce**
A mixture of tomato, spices and vinegar used to pack canned chipotle peppers.

**adzuki beans**
Small reddish-brown beans that are popular in Japan. They are easily digestible.

**apple cider vinegar**
Made from fermented apples, this vinegar has an abundance of potassium and also contains malic acid, which aids in digestion. White vinegar is acidic and harmful to the system, but apple cider vinegar is alkaline and soothing to the system.

**aramé**
A sea vegetable with a mild sea flavour. For more information, see page 17.

**arugula**
Also referred to as "rocket," this peppery leafy green is great for salads.

**balsamic vinegar**
Pungent and sweet vinegar aged in wooden barrels. Comes in many different grades, from very affordable to very expensive, depending on how long it is aged.

**basmati rice**
A fragrant long-grain rice with nutty taste. Originally from India.

**bok choy**
A member of the cabbage family with green leaves and white stems. Available as a large mature plant, about the size of a head of celery, or in its miniaturized version, as baby bok choy, which is about the size of an adult's hand.

**Bragg's liquid aminos**
A non-fermented, wheat-free all-purpose seasoning made from soybeans and water. It is a good substitute for tamari and soy sauce. Available at health food stores.

**bulgur**
Wheat (with the hull and bran removed) that has been steamed, dried and crushed in small pieces. It is available in either medium or coarse grains.

**capers**
Buds of the caper berry bush. Available packed in brine. Have a salty, marine flavour.

**chipotles**
Smoked jalapenos, available dried or canned with adobo sauce. Smoky, spicy flavour.

**cilantro**
Flavourful herb used in Thai and Mexican cooking. Coriander seeds are the seeds of the cilantro plant.

**dredging**
Lightly dipping a food in crumbs, flour or any kind of coating before cooking.

**gluten flour**
Wheat flour with the starch and bran removed, which results in a high percentage of gluten. Gluten is a protein in wheat that forms a very elastic dough when combined with liquid.

**gochujang**
Korean fermented chili paste with a spicy, pungent flavour. Available at Asian markets.

**hemp seeds**
Hulled seeds of hemp plant that have nutty flavour and are high in protein. Available at health food stores. Should be stored in the fridge. For more information, see page 19.

**hijiki**
A sea vegetable with long string-like strands and a strong sea flavour. For more information, see page 17.

**jasmine rice**
Fragrant long-grain white rice used in Thai cooking.

**kamut**
Ancient grain, suitable for people with wheat allergies.

**lemon grass**
Lemon-scented tropical grass used in Southeast Asian cooking.

**mesclun**
A mixture of young baby lettuce leaves, ideal for salads.

**miso**
Fermented soybean paste. For more information, see page 14.

**msg**
Monosodium glutamate is a controversial flavour enhancer used in many processed foods. Many people have an adverse reaction to MSG.

**nori**
Dark green sea vegetable that comes dried in paper-thin sheets. Most often used as wrapper for sushi.

**polenta**
Traditional Italian staple of cornmeal cooked into a porridge. It can be eaten soft, or allowed to set and then grilled, baked or fried.

**porcini mushrooms**
Intensely flavoured mushrooms, most often available dry; must be soaked before use. Porcini is the Italian name; in France, the same mushrooms are called "cèpes."

**rice vinegar**
Made from fermented rice, it has a very mild flavour.

**sambal oelek**
Bright red hot sauce made with red chilies and vinegar. Available at some grocery stores and most Asian markets.

**sea salt**
Salt derived from evaporated sea water.

**shiitake mushrooms**
Japanese mushrooms with an earthy flavour. Available fresh or dried.

**soba**
Light-brown Japanese noodles made from either buckwheat or buckwheat and wheat flours.

**soft silken tofu**
A soft custard-like form of soybean curd that is silky in texture and mild in flavour.

**spelt**
Wheat-like grain that is tolerated by most people with wheat intolerance. Available as whole grains or as flour.

**tahini**
Paste of ground sesame seeds.

**tamari**
Naturally brewed Japanese soy sauce. For more information, see page 14.

**tempeh**
Fermented soybean cake with a nutty flavour. For more information, see page 13.

**tofu**
Soybean curd pressed into blocks. Very mild flavour. For more information, see page 12.

**udon**
Japanese wheat noodles, available fresh or dried.

**wasabi**
Japanese radish that is dried into a powder, then mixed with water to make a paste. Traditional accompaniment for sushi. Very pungent.

# recommended reading

Balch, Phyllis A., CNC. *Prescription for Nutritional Healing: The A–Z Guide to Supplements.* New York: Avery, 2002.

Calbom, Cherie, and Maureen Keane. *Juicing for Life.* New York: Avery Publishing Group, 1992.

Castorina, Jan, and Dimitra Stais. *Juices: Nature's Cure-all for Health and Vitality.* Boston: Lansdowne Publishing, 1998.

Gagnon, Daniel J. *Liquid Herbal Drops for Everyday Use.* Santa Fe: Botanical Research & Education Institute, 1996.

Graci, Sam. *The Power of Superfoods.* Scarborough, ON: Prentice Hall Canada, 1997.

Juliano. *Raw: The Uncook Book.* New York: HarperCollins, 1999.

McIntyre, Anne. *Drink to Your Health.* New York: Gaia Books, 2000.

Meyerowitz, Steve. *Wheatgrass: Nature's Finest Medicine.* Great Barrington, MA: The Sprout House, 1998.

Murray, Michael, and Joseph Pizzorno. *Encyclopaedia of Natural Medicine.* London: Little Brown and Company, 1990.

Pitchford, Paul. *Healing with Whole Foods: Asian Traditions and Modern Nutrition.* 3rd ed. Berkeley: North Atlantic Books, 2002.

Robbins, John. *Diet for a New America.* Walpole, NH: Still Point Publishing, 1987.

Tal Brown, Ruth. *Juice for Life: Modern Food and Luscious Juice.* Toronto: Macmillan Canada, 2000.

Walker, Norman. *Fresh Fruit and Vegetable Juices. What's Missing in Your Body?* Prescott, AZ: Norwalk Press, 1970.

# acknowledgments

We wish to express our warmest gratitude to Barry Alper, partner and dear friend, for keeping us real with his keen intellect, sharp sense of humour and big heart. You inspire us to give our all and then some.

A big thank you goes to Nicole de Montbrun, our lovely editor at Penguin Books, for seeking us out and guiding us along this most rewarding journey.

We are indebted to the spirited cast of individuals and wonderful characters, both past and present, who have helped make our restaurants remarkable and special. And sincere appreciation to Kennen Kaufmann, Henry Pak, Mogan Subramaniam, J. T. Bush, Laura (Fred) Pitchford, Yasemin Zorlutuna, Deborah Hochman, Amanda Hardman, Sarah Attwell, Rebecca Morrison, Frances Bell, Juliana Veigh, Cecilia Escobar, Lauren McGuire, Yvonne Moir, Ken Konkle, Vanessa Dunn, Annika Lehmann, Theresa DeGrace, Jessica Martino, Marianne Alas, Jeya Kopalasingam and Prapakaran Gnanasekaram for leading the way.

Carlo Rota, you handsome devil! Thank you for taking the time to write such a lovely and entertaining foreword to this book. You really got it. We would also like to thank photographer and friend Robbie Kane for capturing our Fresh spirit with his camera lens in the authors' photo. Thank you Richard Brooks, photographer and man of many talents for shooting the Fresh locations in action.

We are so thankful for the decadent dessert recipes contributed by Eden Hertzog, Shoshana Gehring and Ilana Kadonoff. You have definitely raised the bar for vegan baking in this city.

In our business we have the great privilege of working closely with many interesting, creative and wonderful people. Over the past few years, these people have made a positive and lasting contribution to Fresh and Juice for Life: Nancy DeCaria for signage, bookkeeping and being an all-around great gal; Cary Laudadio, Brian Wilcox and Ken Randall for our graphics; Ezra and Peter at

Canada Food Equipment for all our equipment needs; Leo Downey, the "Juicer Doctor"; Raymond Jareckas, the "fridge guy"; Michael at Mak Imaging; Louie at Nikolaou; Dee at Tap Phong; Markus Grossman for painting; Tony Goslinsky, Michael Tucker and everyone at Crown Taxi; Marie at Super Sprouts; Connie and Paul at the Ontario Natural Food Co-op; Rich Donsky at Mr. Produce; Sergio Milani at Bruzzi Food Services; Rich Brown for pitching in and getting the job done, no matter how big or small; and Ivan LeCouvie of LeCouvie Construction for building and fixing and building and fixing and ...

Big hugs for our dream team: Ralph Giannone, Pina Petricone and Jason Smirnis of Giannone Associates Architects Inc. for designing our most beautiful and functional space ever at Fresh on Crawford.

Finally, we are awed and grateful for myriad dear and loyal customers who walk through our doors each day to enjoy the fruits of our labours. Thank you so much.

*RTB & JLH*

## on a personal note

Deep appreciation to Rich Brown for your rock-steady encouragement, warm love and determined support over the past seven years and throughout the intense writing of this book. You have my heart.

Much love to my stepsons, Marley and Haile Brown, for being so cool and easygoing with me and for keeping the volume down so I could work on this book.

To my cherished family—my mom and dad, David and Vered Tal; Ronnie and Vicky Tal; Iris and Michael Halbert; Alma Brown; Richard Lee Brown; and Janice and Byron Ward. Big hugs to all my nieces and nephews—Carly, Jeremy, Ari, Jonah, Adam, Naftali, Shalom, Leyah, Adina, Yoel, Chondra and David.

Friends I treasure—Alison (Juicy Lucy); Owen; Rhonda Moscoe; Jane Miller; Lisa Kelner; Bonnie Beacher; Robyn Levy; Diane Bruni; Jane Loney; Danny Paradise; Micha and Liat (Kibbutz Nir-David) Levy; Richard and Diane Brooks; Stash Golas; Akasha Kat Nilson and Tyler Nilson; Carlo Rota and Kathryn Zenna; Robbie,

Sylvana, Sophie, Shanah and Gypsy; Jana Lynn and Vince John Vincent; and finally, Maya One Drop (the Great Dane).

Thank you, Greg Moyer, for inspiring me to go vegan and for taking the first steps with me on this juicy journey 13 years ago. Thank you, Michael Bessen, for being the angel with deep pockets, saving my butt and giving me a future to look forward to. Thank you lovely songbirds Kate Fenner, Lorraine Segato and Michelle MacAdorey for lending a hand in the early days.

Juice bars and eateries that have hugely inspired me along the way and are always worth a special visit: Lucky's Juice Joint (New York City), Juicy Lucy's (Vancouver), Re-Bar (Victoria), Juice Lab (Nosara, Costa Rica), Gravity Bar (Seattle), Angelica's Kitchen (New York City), Spirite Lounge (Montreal), Fluide (Mont Tremblant) and Making Waves and Living Seed (Toronto).

Books and authors that have inspired and informed me are *The Power of Superfoods* (Sam Graci), *Juicing for Life* (Cherie Calbom), *Raw* (Juliano), *Healing with Whole Foods* (Paul Pitchford), *Fit for Life* (Harvey Diamond), *The ReBar Cookbook* (Audrey Alsterberg), *Angelica's Kitchen Cookbook* (Leslie McEachern) and *The Millennium Cookbook* (Eric Tucker and John Westerdahl).

Jen, thank you for agreeing to come along on this journey. You are brilliant, funny, beautiful and amazing in the kitchen! You have become an integral ingredient in our recipe for success.

*Peace, RTB*

Many thanks to my family—my parents, Libo, Nana and Gannin, Aunty Pen and family, and Aunty Betty—a.k.a. Wayne, Barbara and Elizabeth Houston; Phyllis and Jim White; Penelope, Gary, Jeff and Amanda Warner; and Betty Robinson. Also to my many aunts, uncles and cousins in Wallaceburg and Chatham.

To my friends—Kim Thompson (you rock × 3), Christine MacLachlan, Dave Wright, Katie Hitchmough, Melissa Curcumelli-Rodostamo, Jessica Grant, Jojo Stewart, Mary Lynn Turk, Gabrielle Shaw, Erin Best, Heidi McKee (my Queen's gourmet cooking partner) and my best friend of all, Rachel Rose.

Thanks to everyone who has made cooking so much fun over the years. To Sue Bruton, Benji Perosin and Marg Hitchcock from the Wellington; Quade Generoux, Chris Pirie, Jeremy Smith and Tara Mills from Moorelands Camp; James Russell Los Binnie, Scott Murden, Lori Kilback and Andrew Field from JFL; and Maria Hutton from George Brown.

And to Ruth—I feel very lucky to have you in my life and to get to work with you every day. When I think back on the two of us working on this project, all I remember is the laughs!

*JLH*

# index

notes

notes

notes